COLUMBIA ROAD

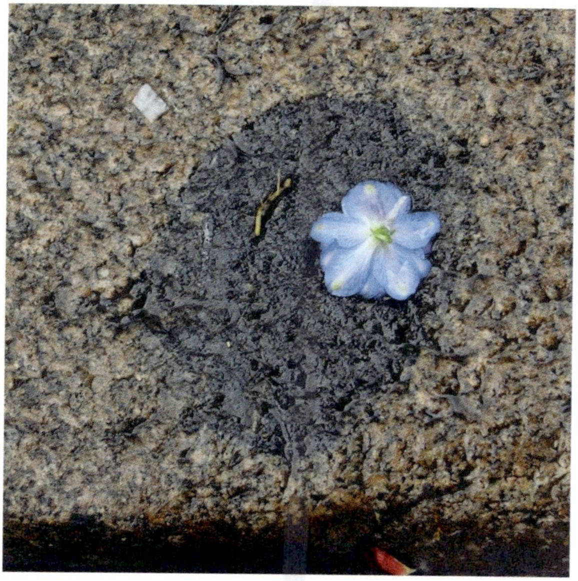

COLUMBIA ROAD

by Johanna Neurath

HOXTON MINI PRESS

Book One
I've Lived in East London for 86½ Years

Book Two
East London Swimmers

Book Three
A Portrait of Hackney

Book Four
Shoreditch Wild Life

Book Five
One Day Young in Hackney

Book Six
Drivers in the 1980s

Book Seven
Columbia Road

East London Photo Stories

Book Seven

INTRODUCTION

Markets have always held a special allure for photographers of urban life. André Kertész documented flower sellers in Paris. Eugène Atget did the same for flea markets. So did Bill Brandt in London. Street photography is about authenticity and improvisation. It's about embracing the everyday and the unexpected. It's about chucking yourself, camera-first, into the throng and seeing where it takes you. And what better spot to do this than a market? Like a touring theatre, it roars in at dawn, transforming the street into a makeshift stage, festooned with eye-catching wares, peopled by a cast of boisterous barrow boys, meandering tourists, curious locals, savvy regulars. A proper slice of the city – which, by the end of the day, is gone.

Every Sunday, Columbia Road in Hackney is home to London's biggest dedicated flower market. Originally a path used to transport cattle down to Smithfield's slaughterhouses, by the mid 19th century the area had become a slum. In 1869, philanthropist Angela Burdett-Coutts bought the land and redeveloped it, building a covered food market there. Initially the flower market ran on a Saturday but later switched to a Sunday to suit the East End's many Jewish vendors. Head down that way now and you'll find stallholders whose market lineage goes back generations, as well as a newer contingent of Hackneyites selling flat whites, vintage fashion or graphic art from the Victorian shops that line the street.

Shot over a decade, Johanna's images capture the joyful humour and energy of the market. The kaleidoscope of flora. Shopping bags brimming with goods. Abstract patterns reflected in windows. A little dog. You can almost feel yourself being jostled around, almost hear the traders' patter around you. But this isn't that brash, in-your-face school of street photography – in fact, few faces are visible. Johanna's approach glories in random moments of harmony between colour, texture, light and form. People are almost incidental, neat visual echoes for the foliage – the green sweets they eat and green trousers they wear resemble plant stalks. In this resolutely democratic frame, a shoe-clad foot isn't automatically more important than a polystyrene cup simply because it happens to have a human attached.

Come 3pm, as the market closes and petals congregate like snow, or confetti, on the floor, Johanna turns her lens on what's left behind. Flowers and leaves, scraps of shiny packaging and bright orange netting, scattered across the floor or floating serenely in buckets of water, become captivating still lifes. Traditionally the still life gives an artist license to organise a set of objects very deliberately. In vanitas paintings flowers feature in meticulously composed arrangements of skulls, fruit and other objects intended to symbolise the fleeting nature of life. More recently, photographers Robert Mapplethorpe and Irving Penn took elegant, close-up still lifes of flowers against plain backdrops. And with the still lifes of contemporary advertising, every effort is made to emphasise perfection and convince us we should buy the product.

What Johanna presents appears at first to be the opposite of all this. The mess, the detritus, the odds and ends that couldn't possibly be sold. And yet they're beautiful. Henri Cartier-Bresson, himself no stranger to street markets, said, "Poetry is two elements that are suddenly in conflict." Here, that's the rough, asphalt road, with its cracks and faded yellow markings, or the mucky water, and those delicate, crumpled, still startlingly vibrant petals. Looking at them, we remember that these are not living organisms. They're cut flowers, dead plants. Maybe we're not so far from the vanitas. After all, the French words for still life are "nature morte". Johanna directs our attention to something we'd normally ignore or trample underfoot without a thought. She elevates it. A reminder that there's poetry to be found in the least likely places.

Rachel Segal Hamilton

PHOTOGRAPHER'S NOTE

It's my Sunday ritual, a weekly "walking and looking" meditation on chance, chaos and chrysanthemums. I head due south a few minutes down Queensbridge Road, cross the Hackney Road (I like that it's known as *THE* Hackney Road), past the pubs serving Sunday Roasts and down to the street which is paved with gold, pink and green.

The stallholders know me there now. I'm that crazy lady who takes pictures of the gutters of Columbia Road Flower Market, once the worst of the crowds have gone. I get in their way as they pack up – they're eager to get everything tidied away into their vans before going off to the pub or heading back home for late lunches.

For more than ten years, and more or less every weekend come rain or shine (rain makes for nicer photographs) I've been wandering down Columbia Road camera in hand to record the riot of colour and pattern left on the ground. Petals, leaves, old fag butts, polystyrene tea cups are trampled and squashed underfoot into a delicious street salad. The visuals are almost edible. The flower buckets hold tasty soups of the day: cherry blossom soup in the spring and hot red berries a favourite for winter.

Once everything's been sold, given away or tipped out on the ground, the scavengers circle and descend to quarrel over the rich pickings. I'm in there too – not that I ever take any of the greenery or flowers home. I look but never touch. I'm simply interested in what's been recorded by my camera.

Johanna Neurath

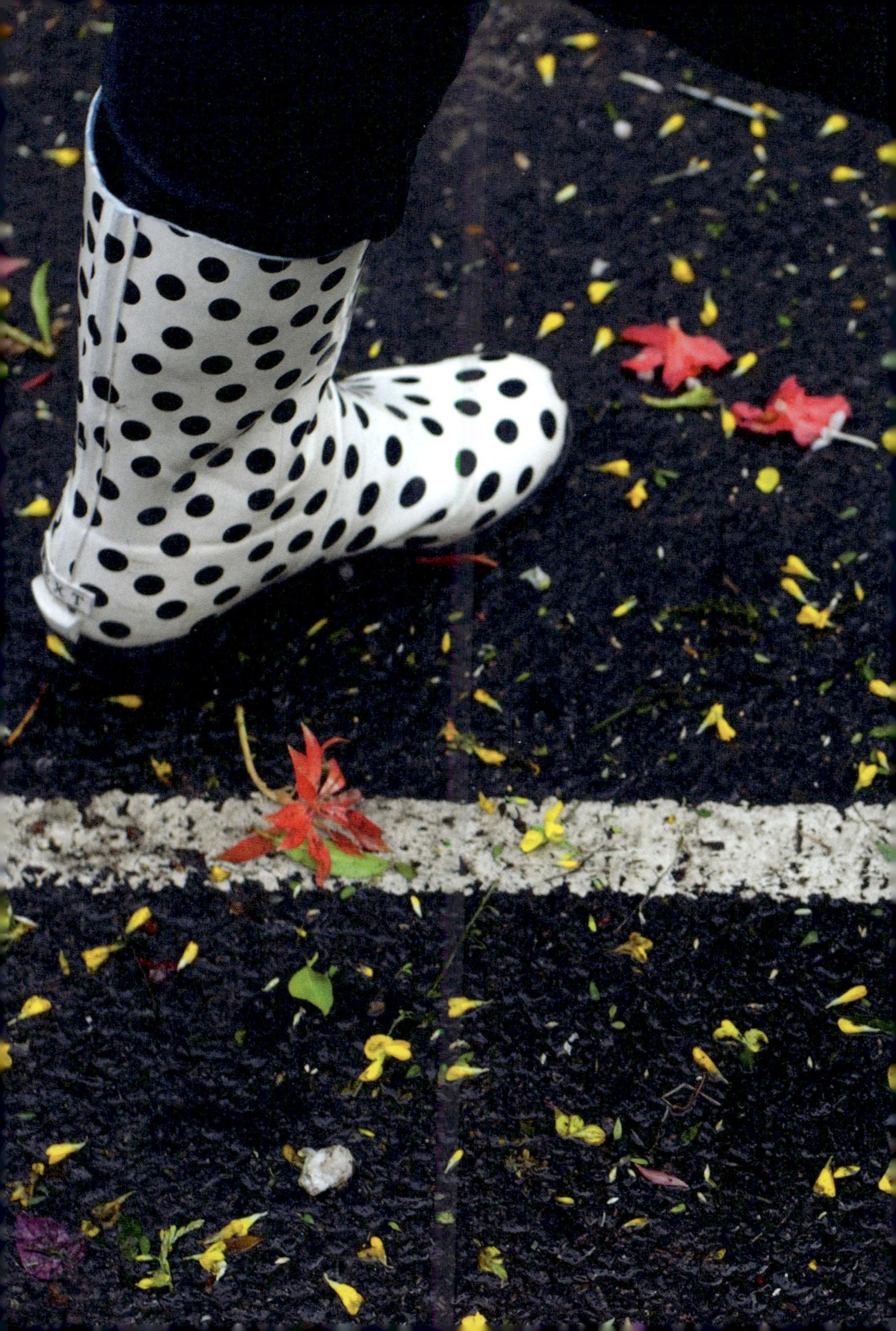

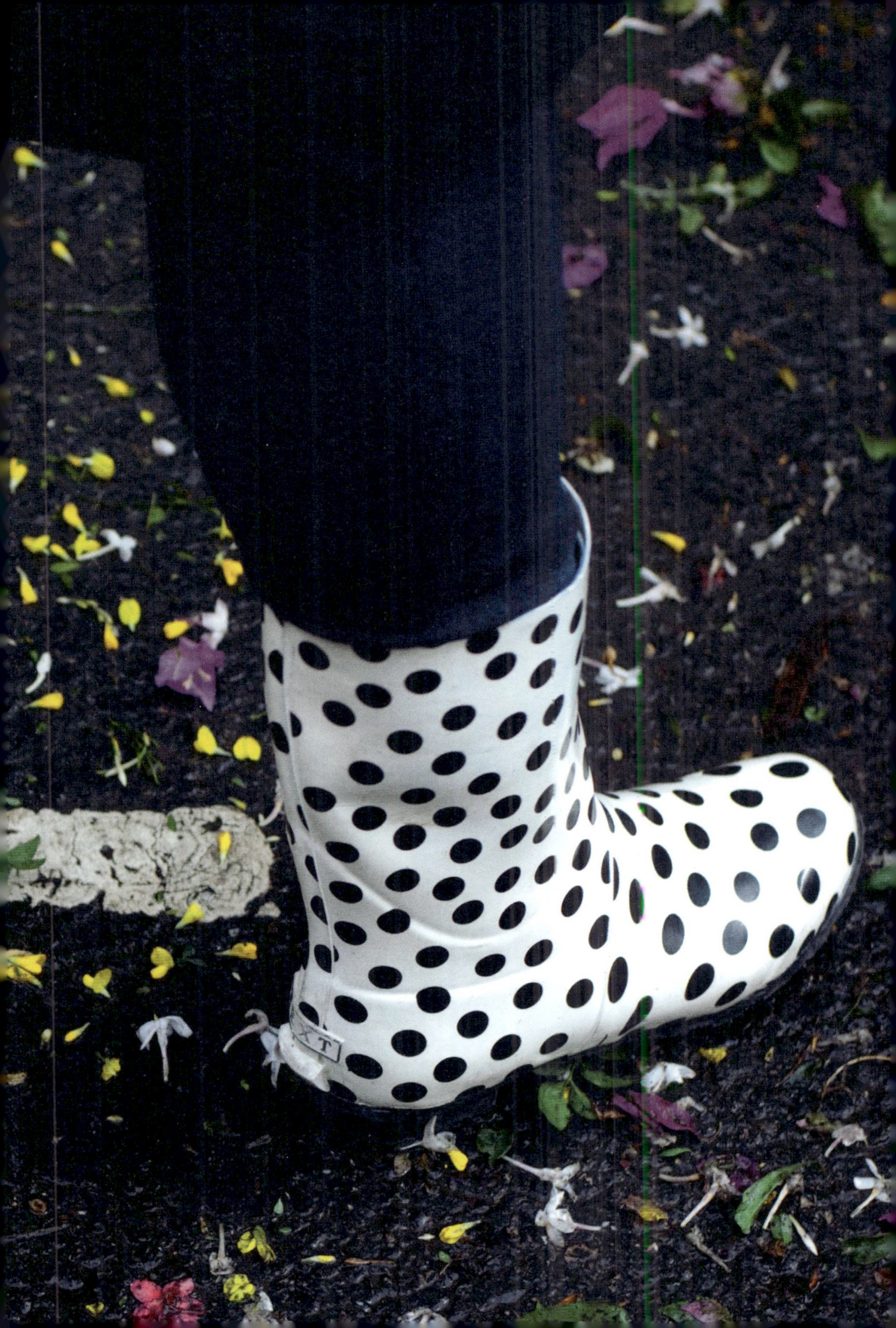

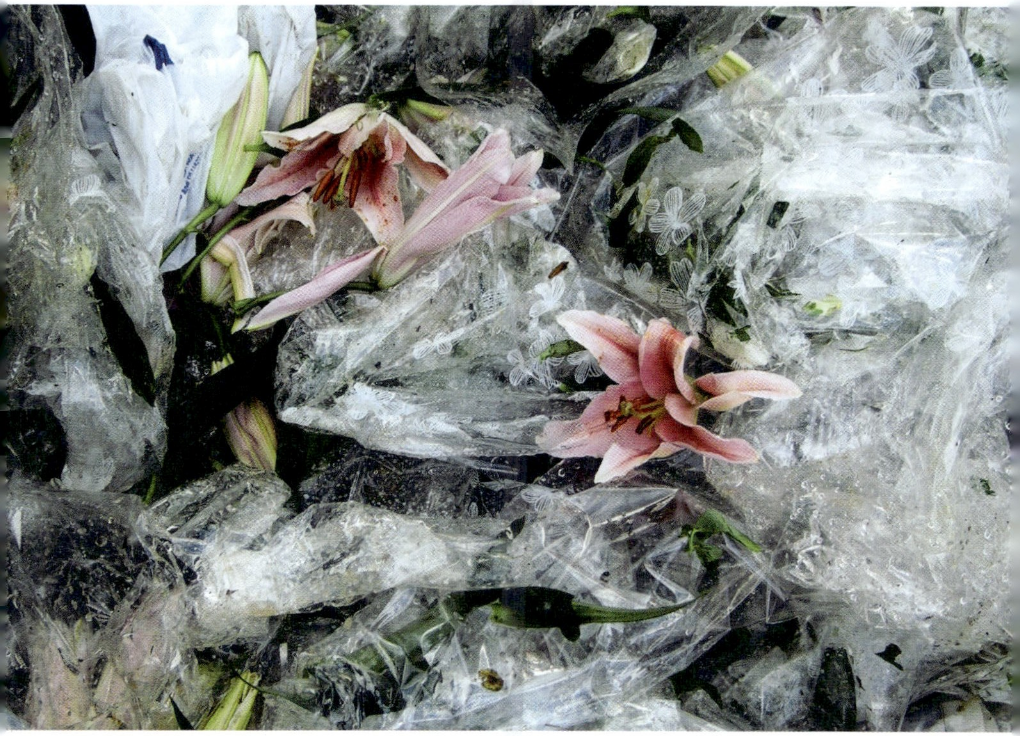

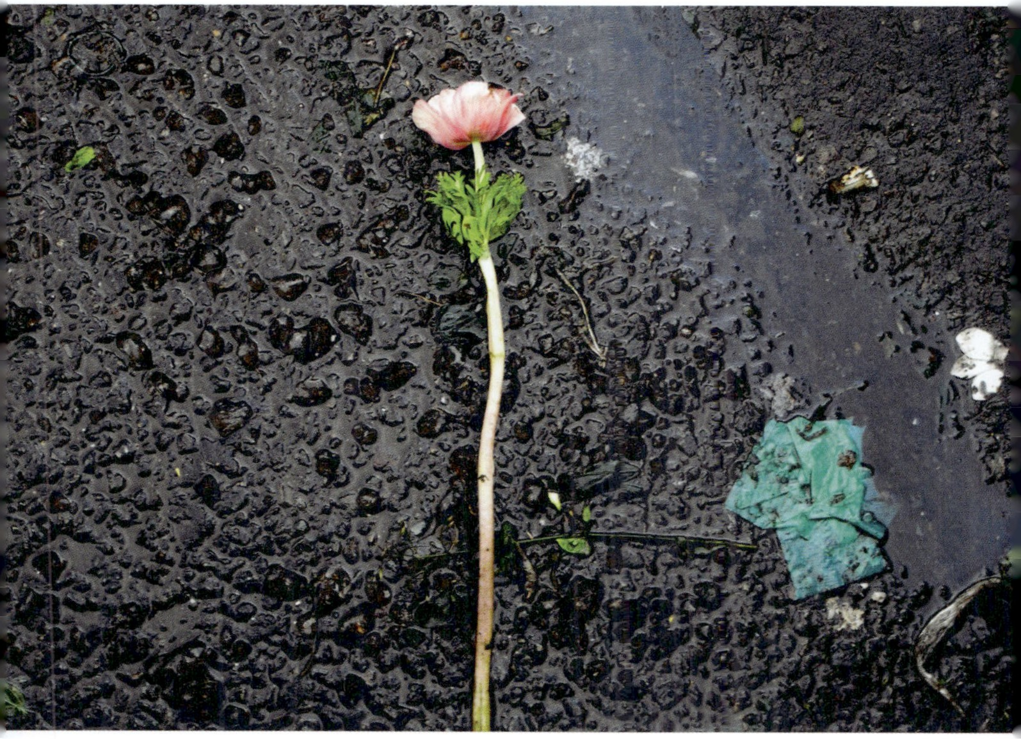

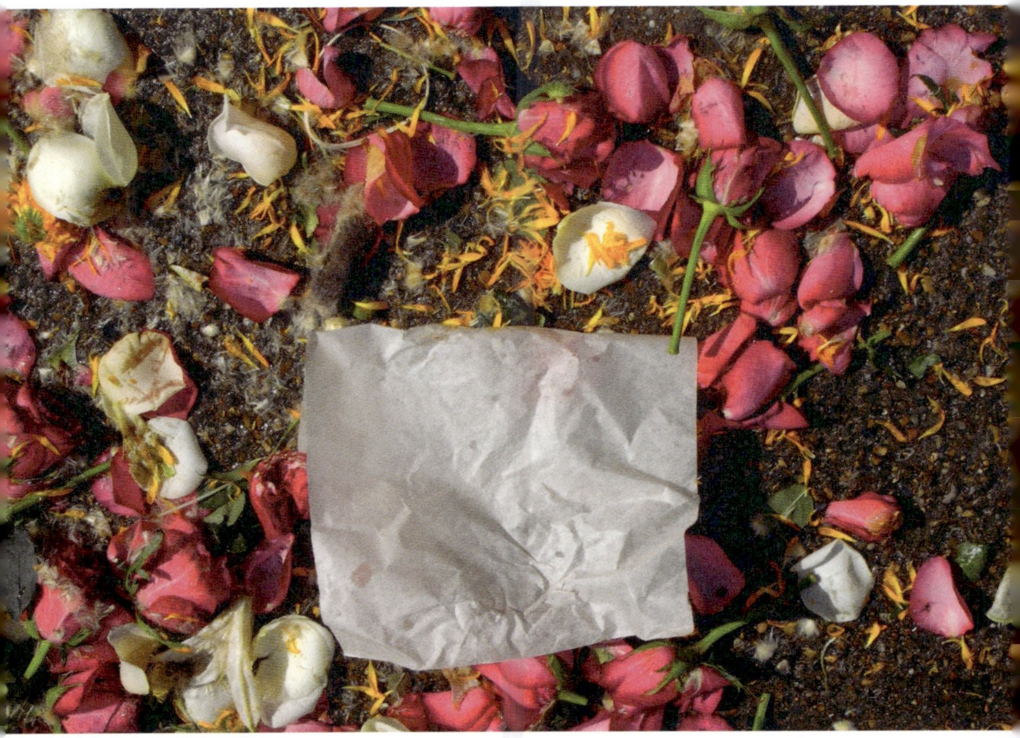

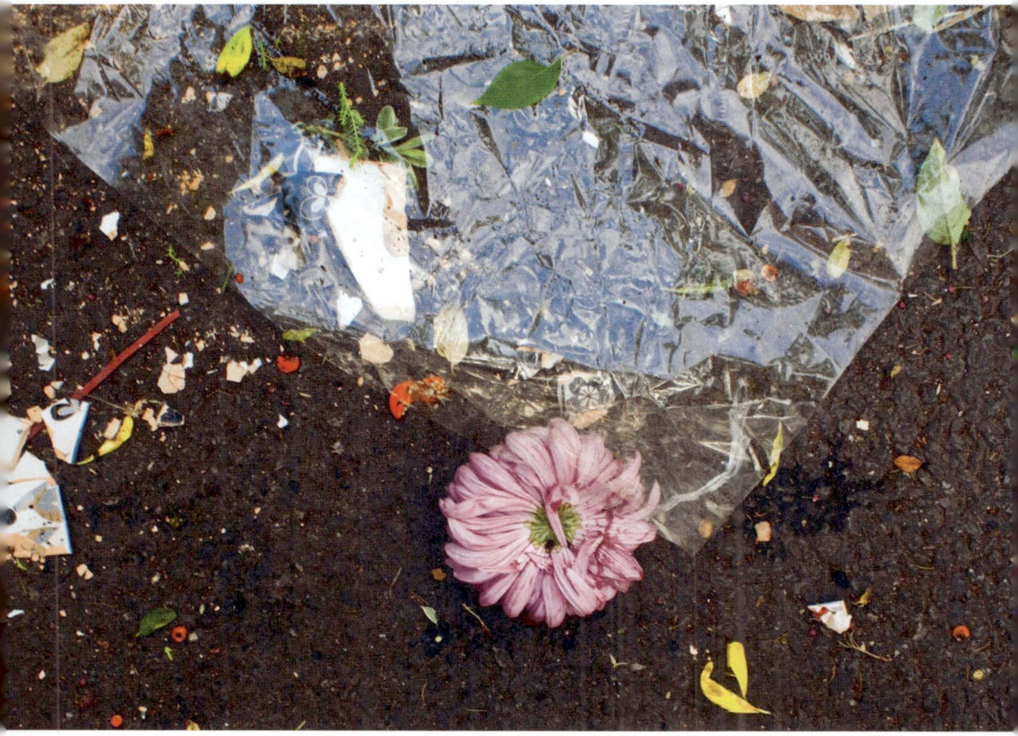

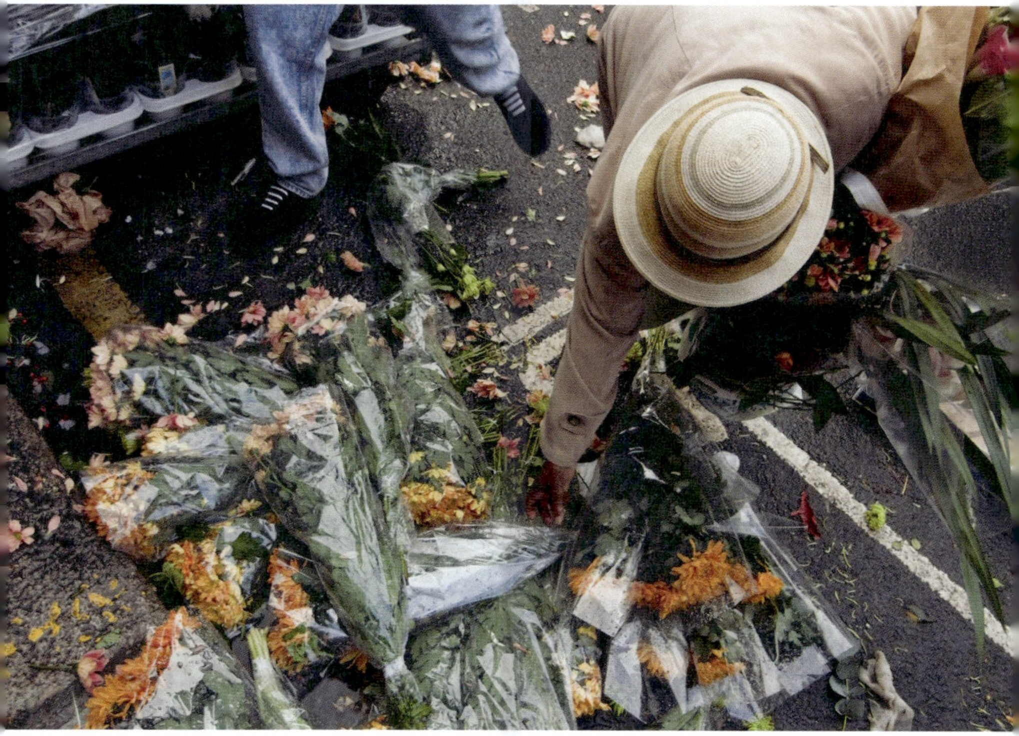

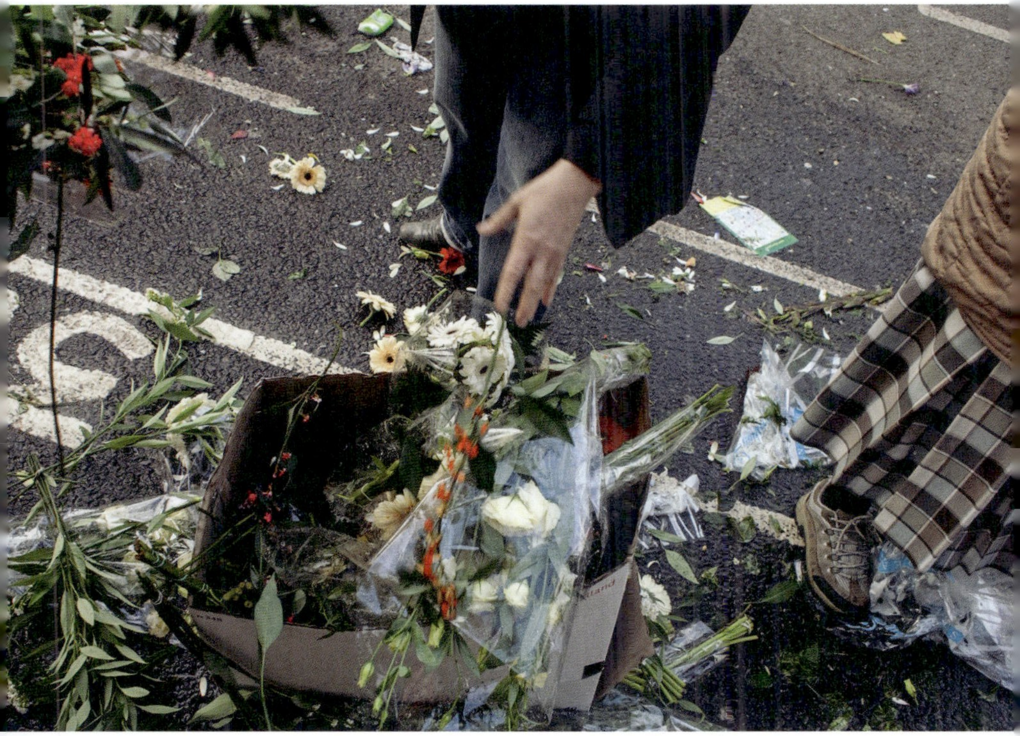

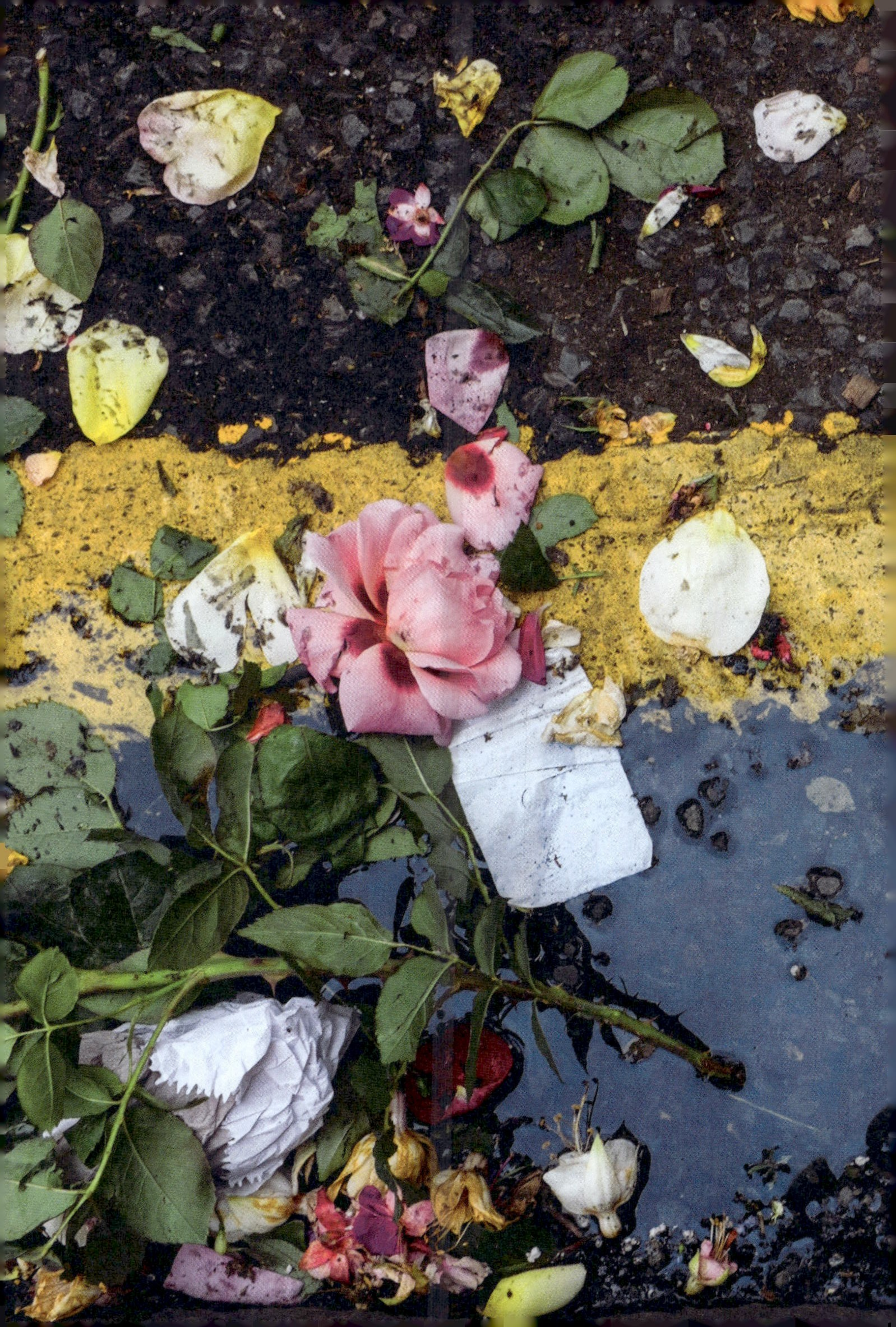

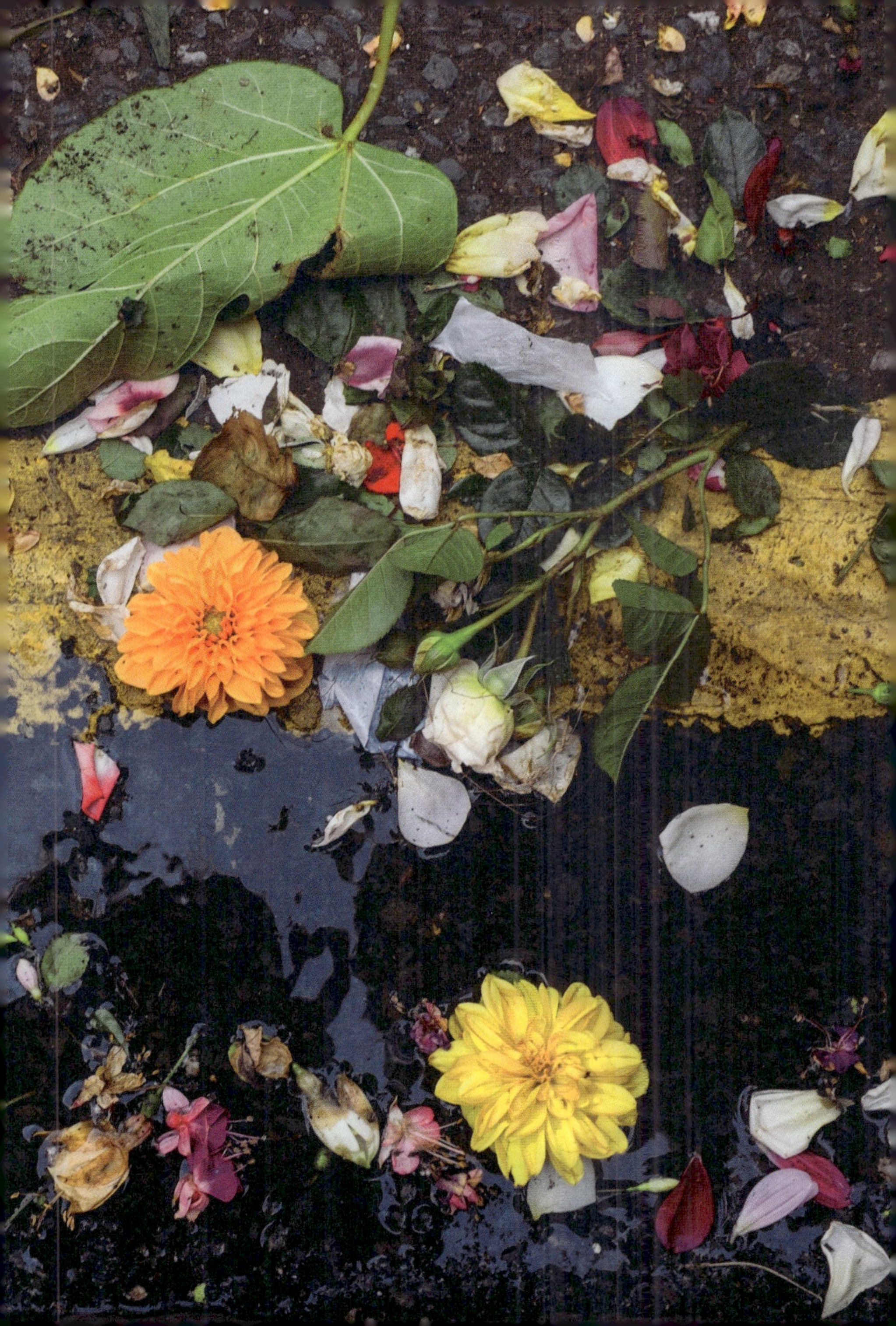

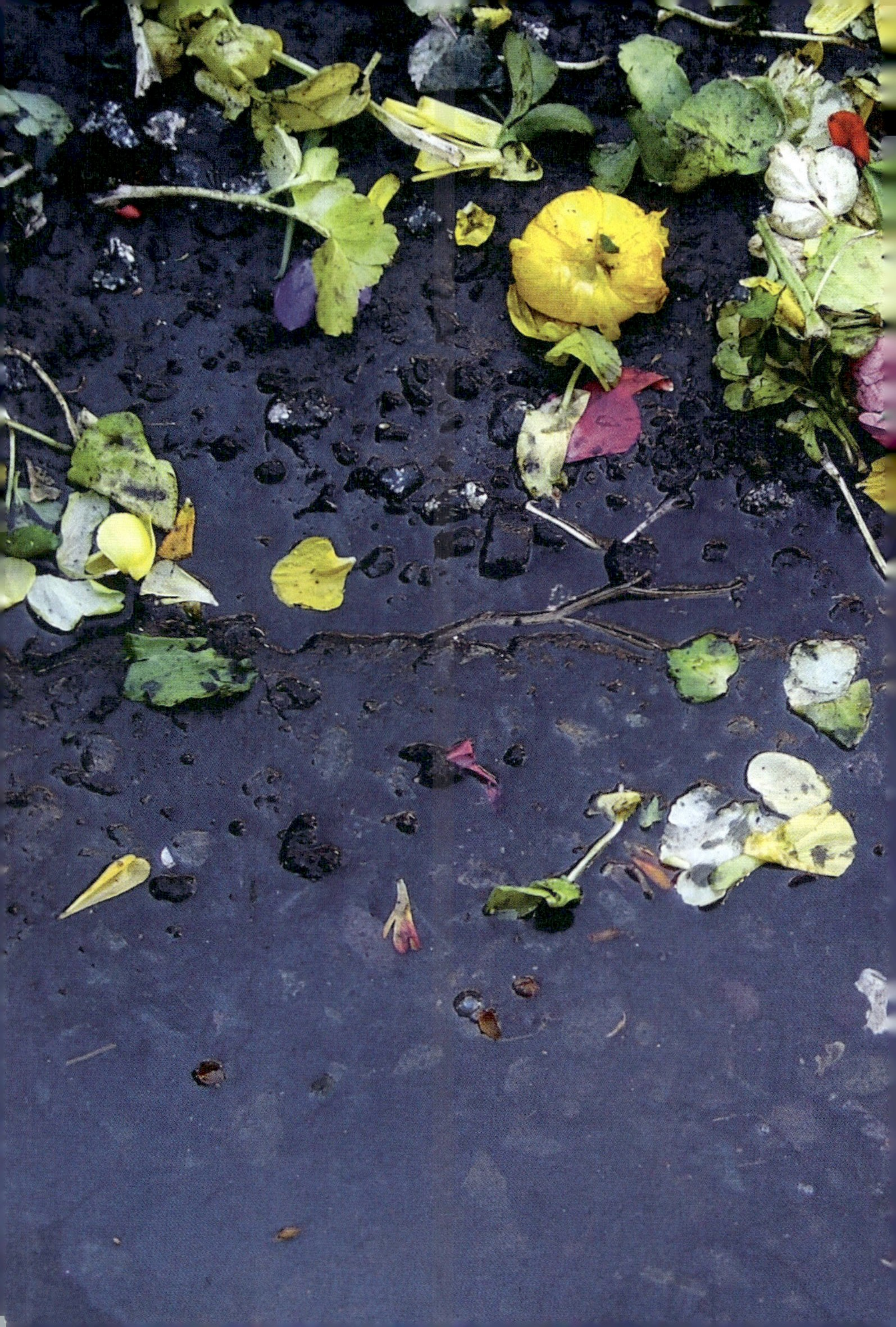

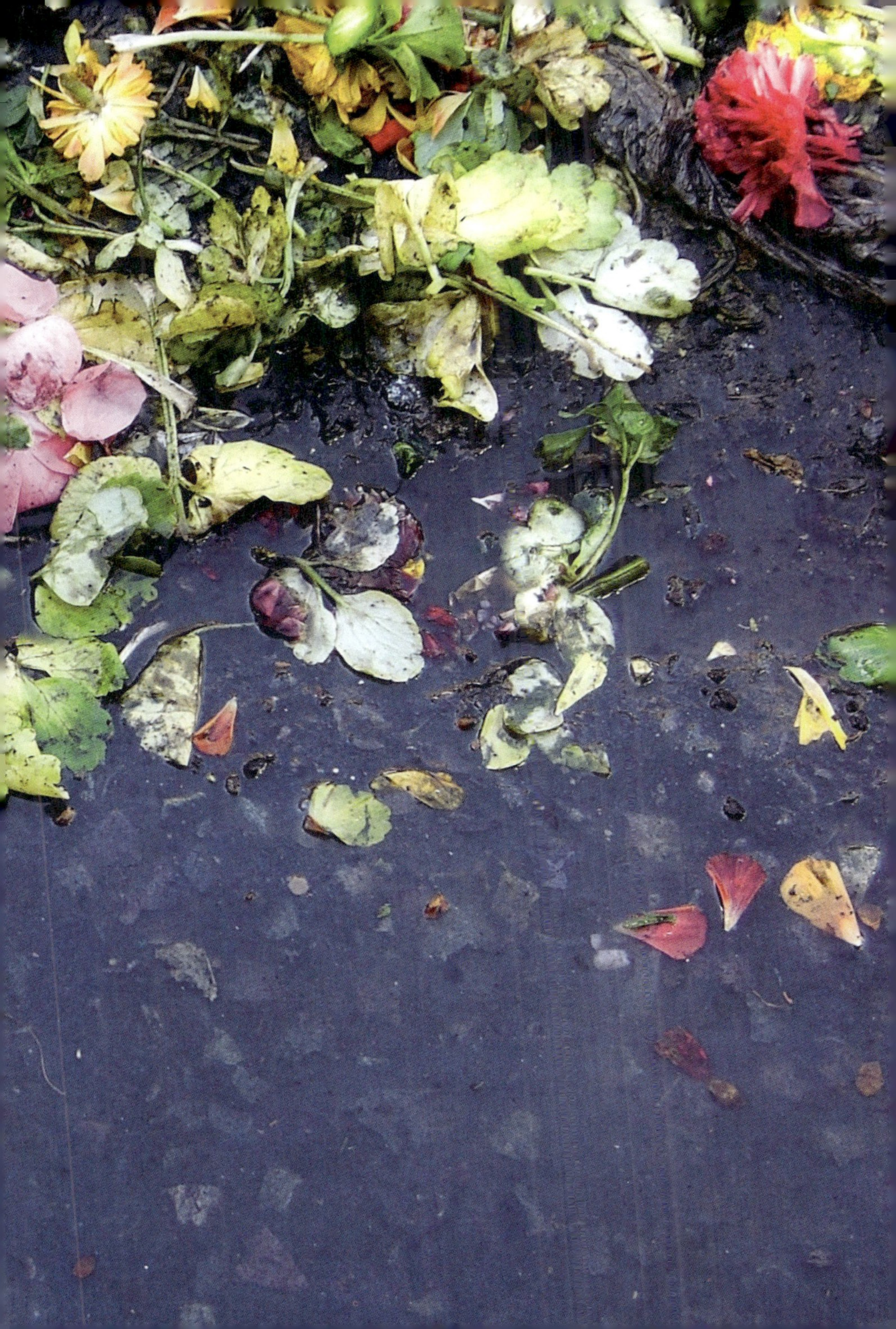

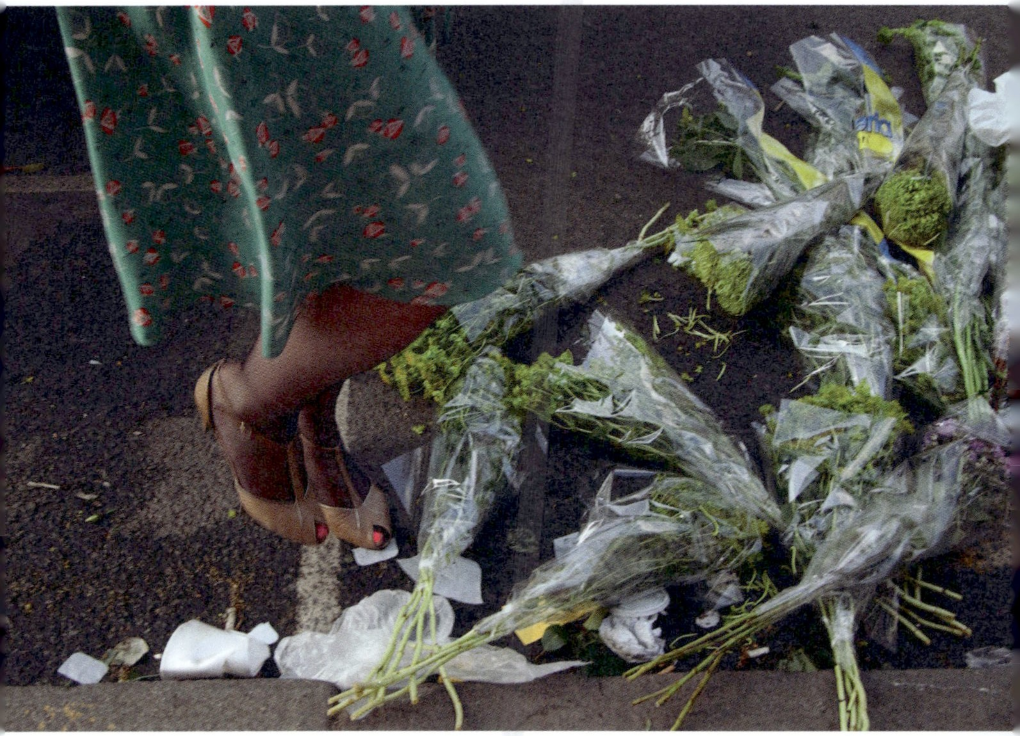

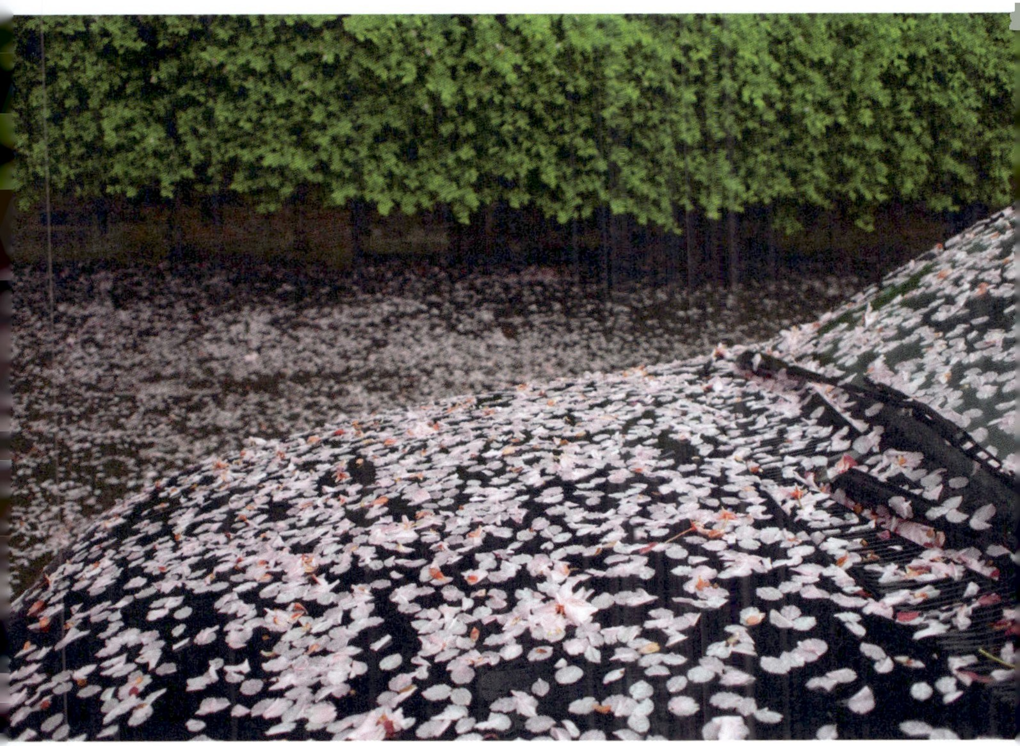

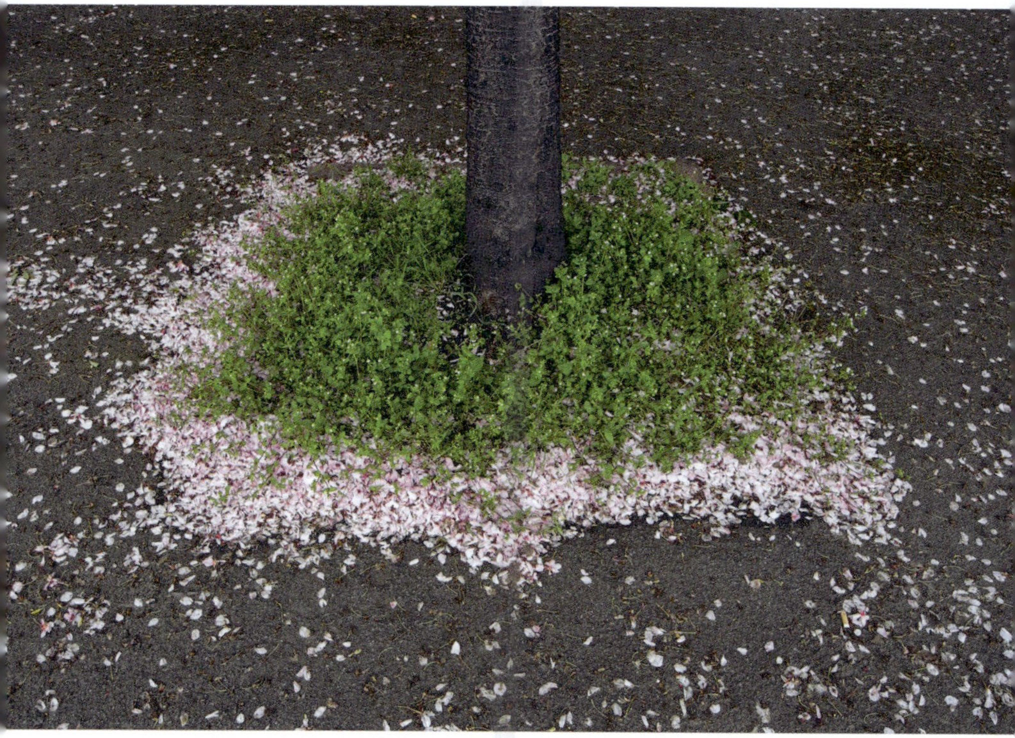

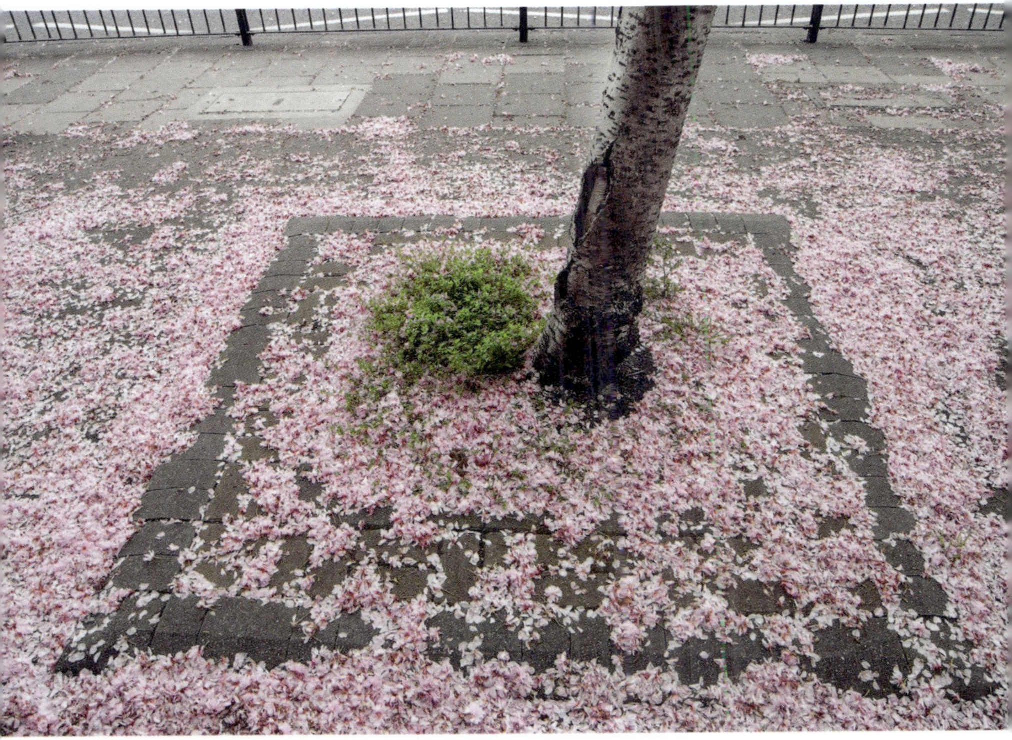

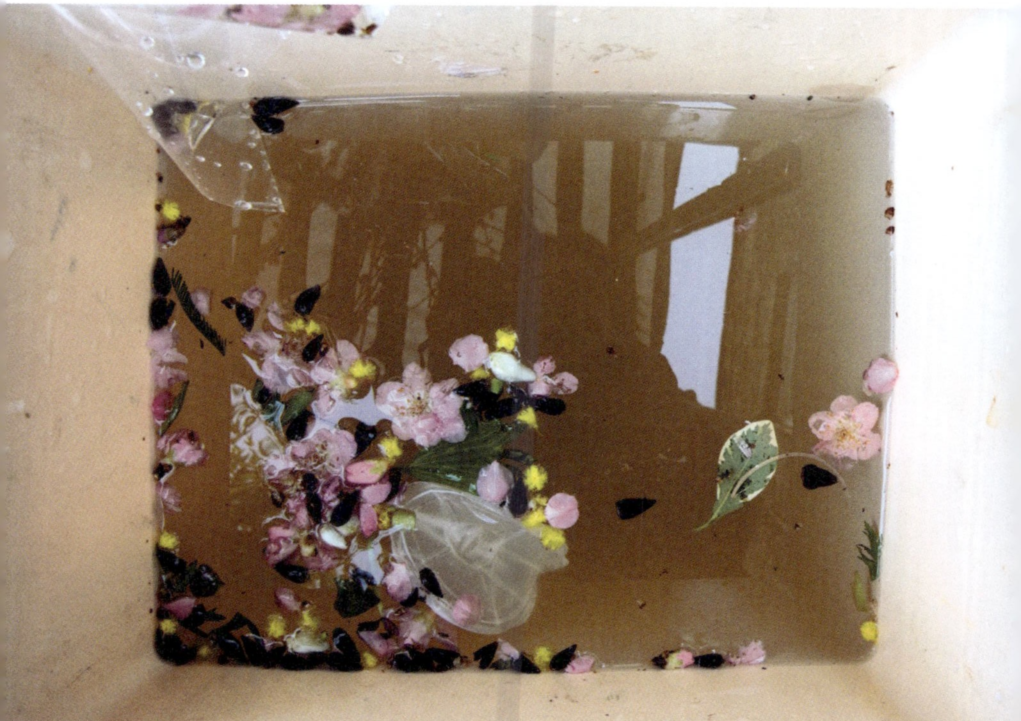

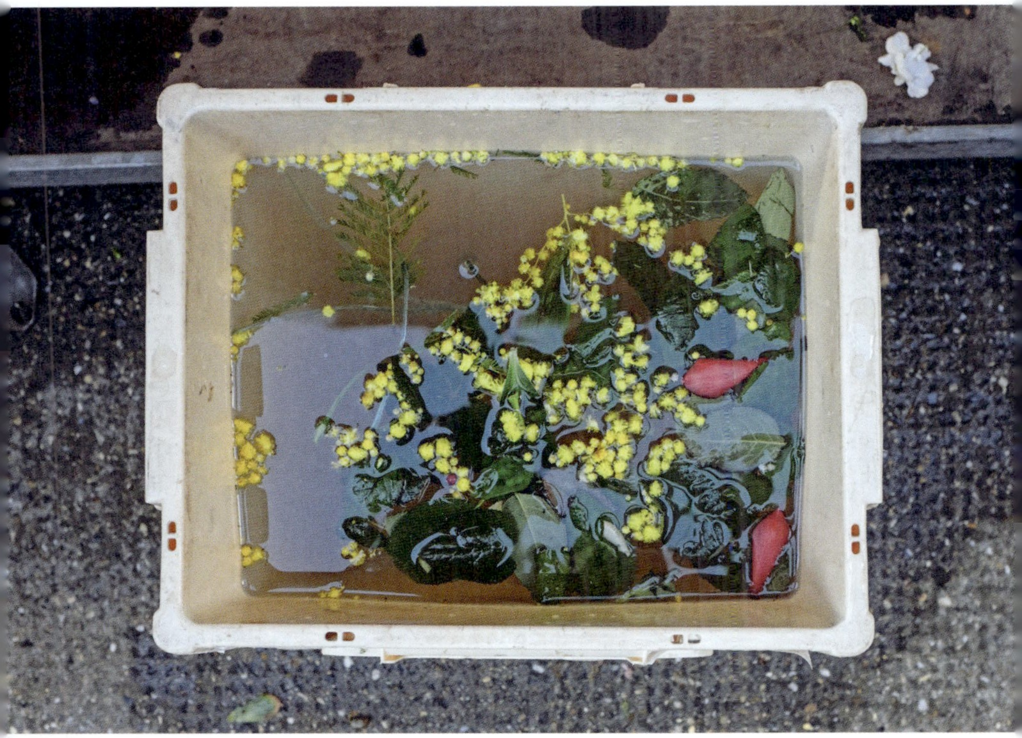

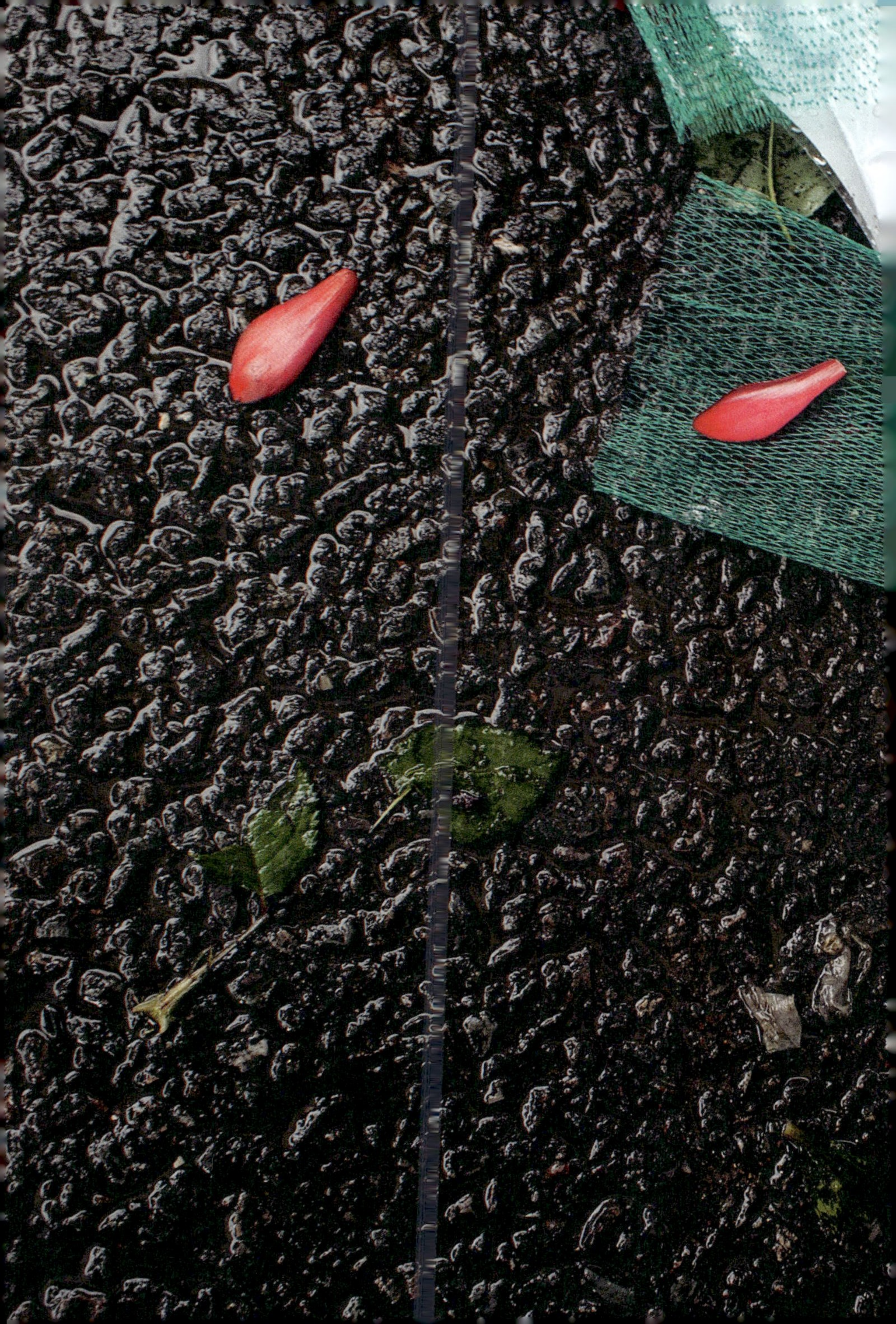

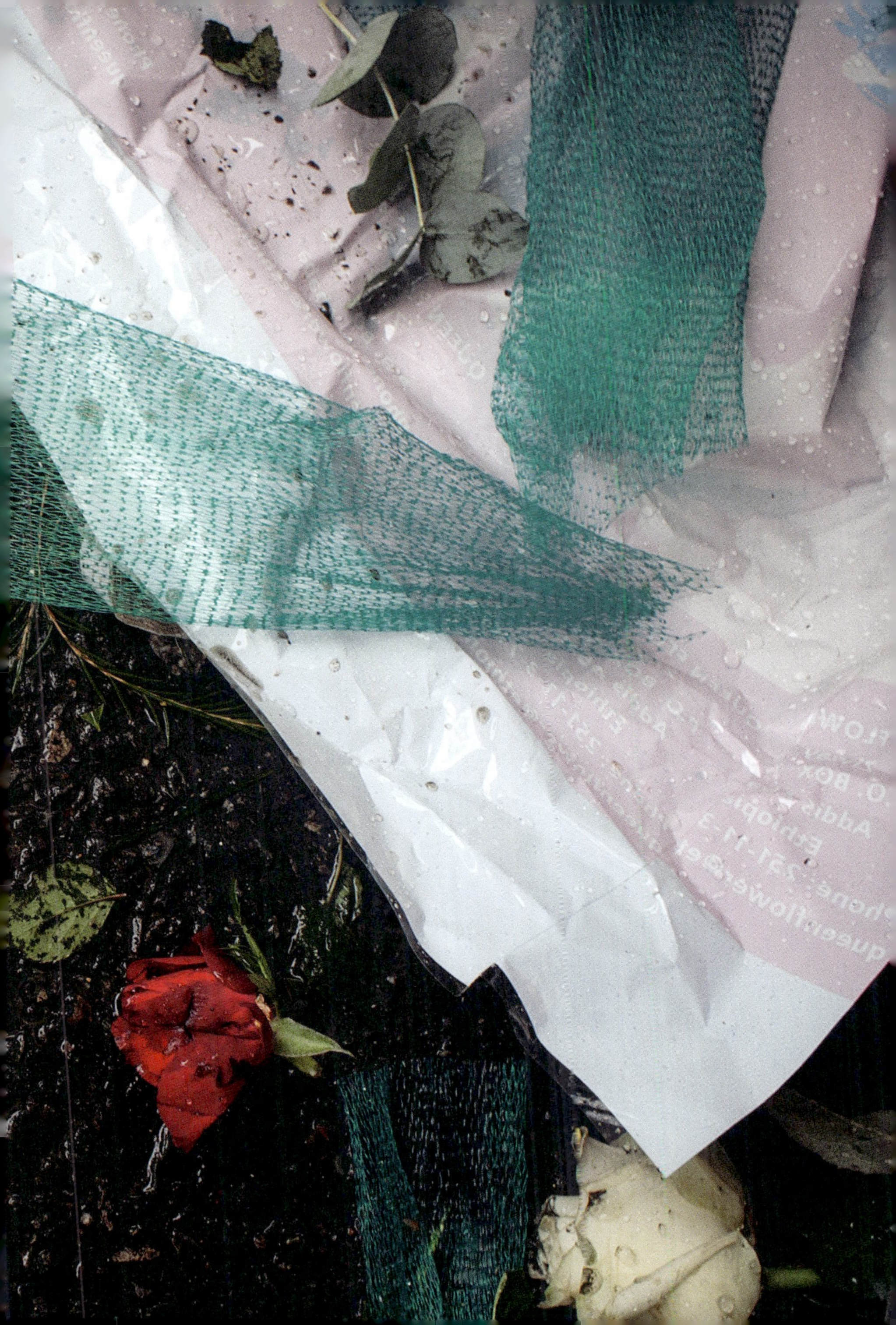
Addis

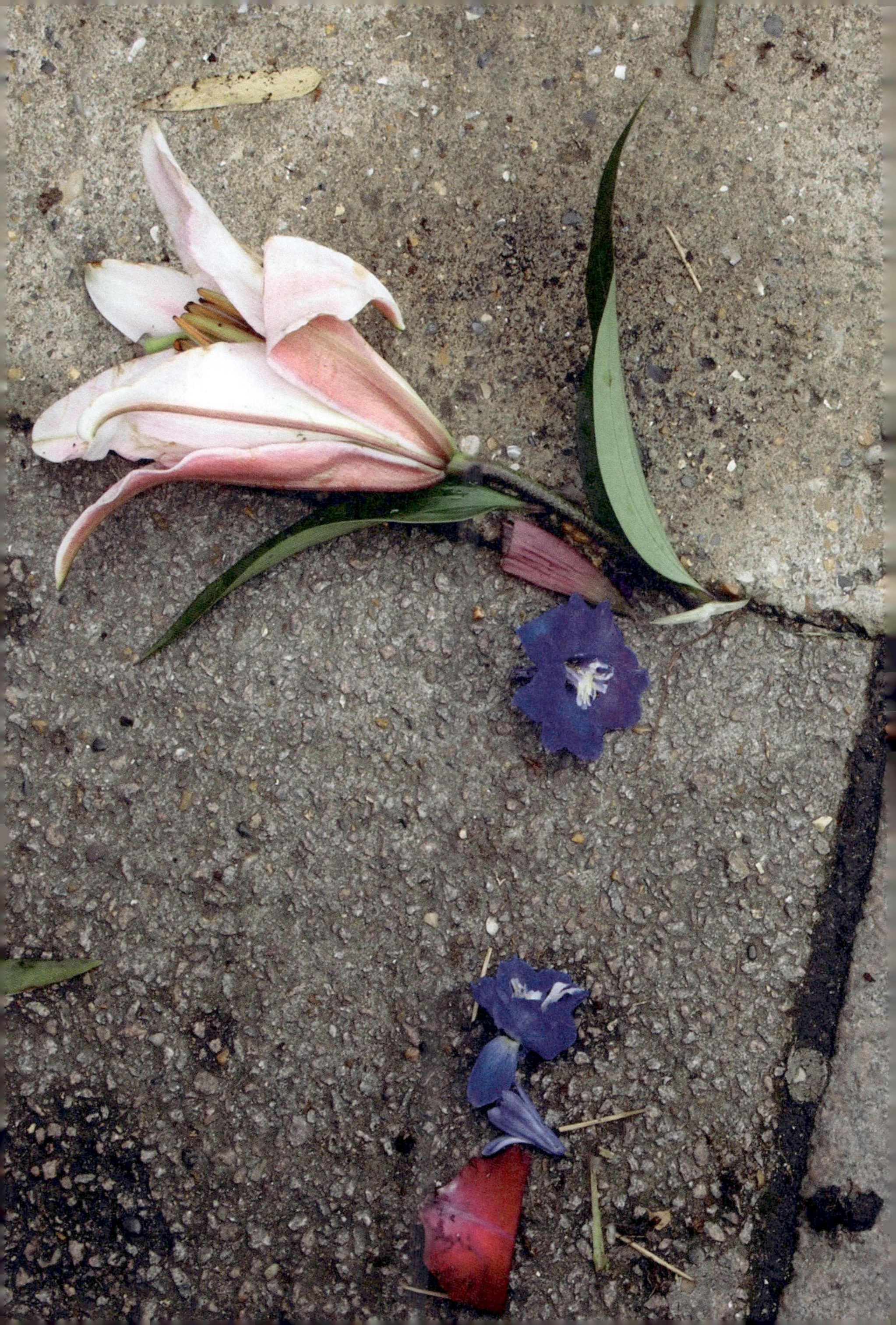

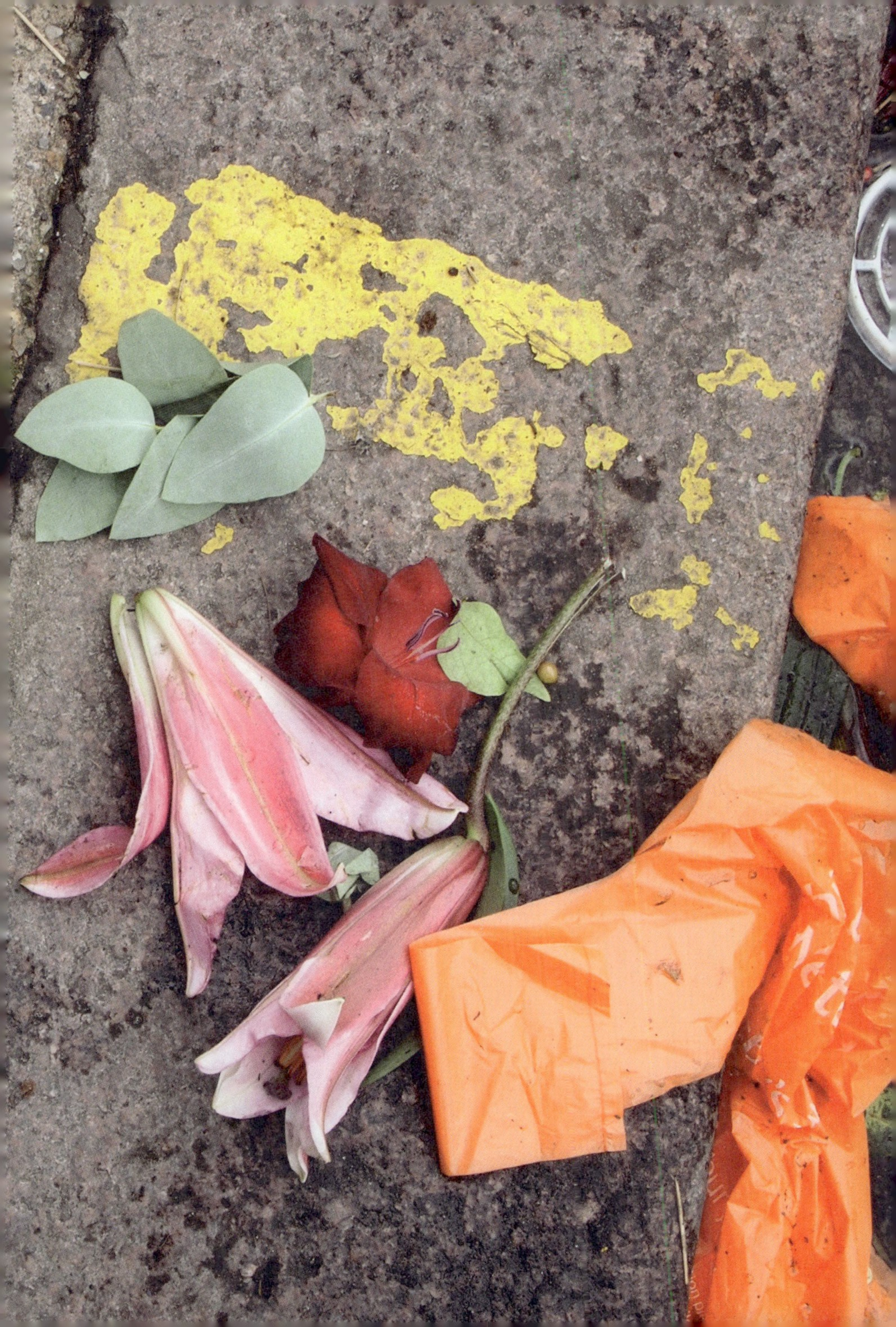

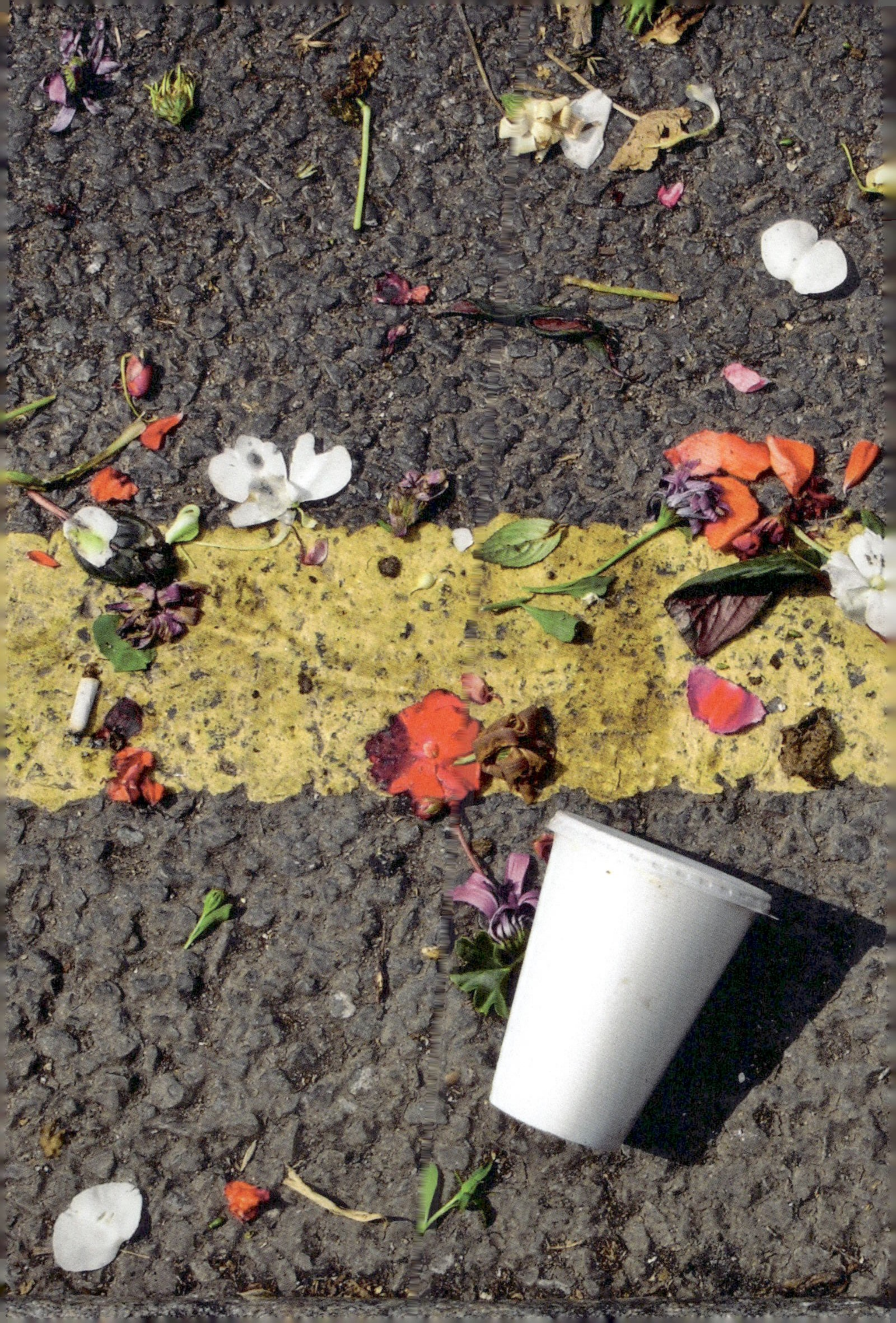

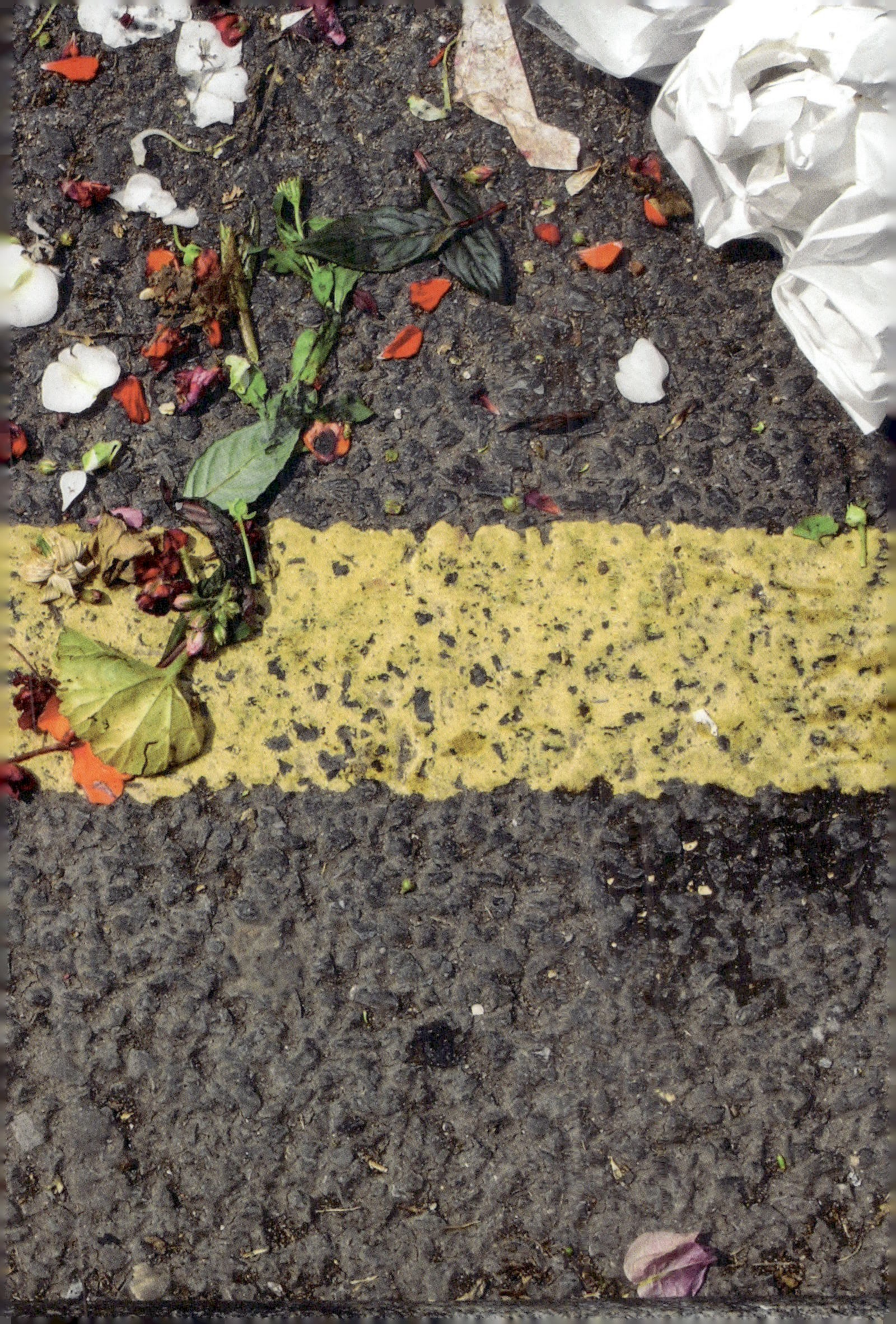

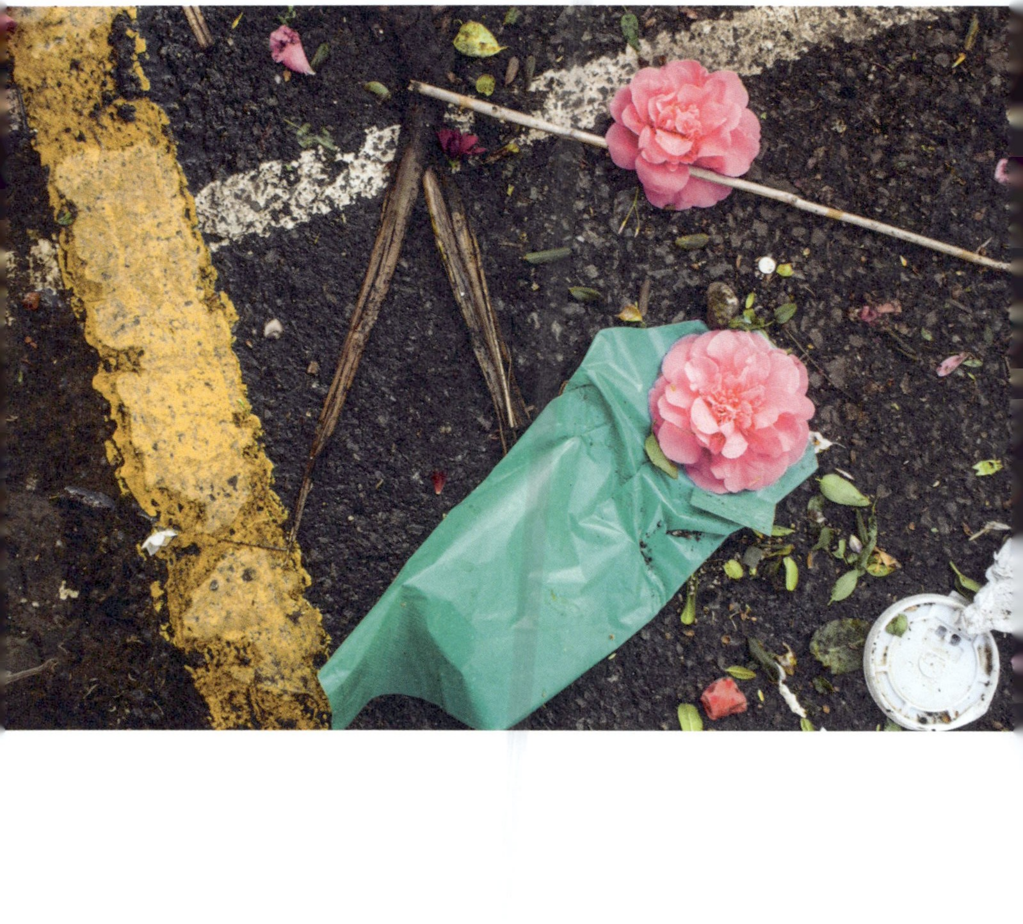

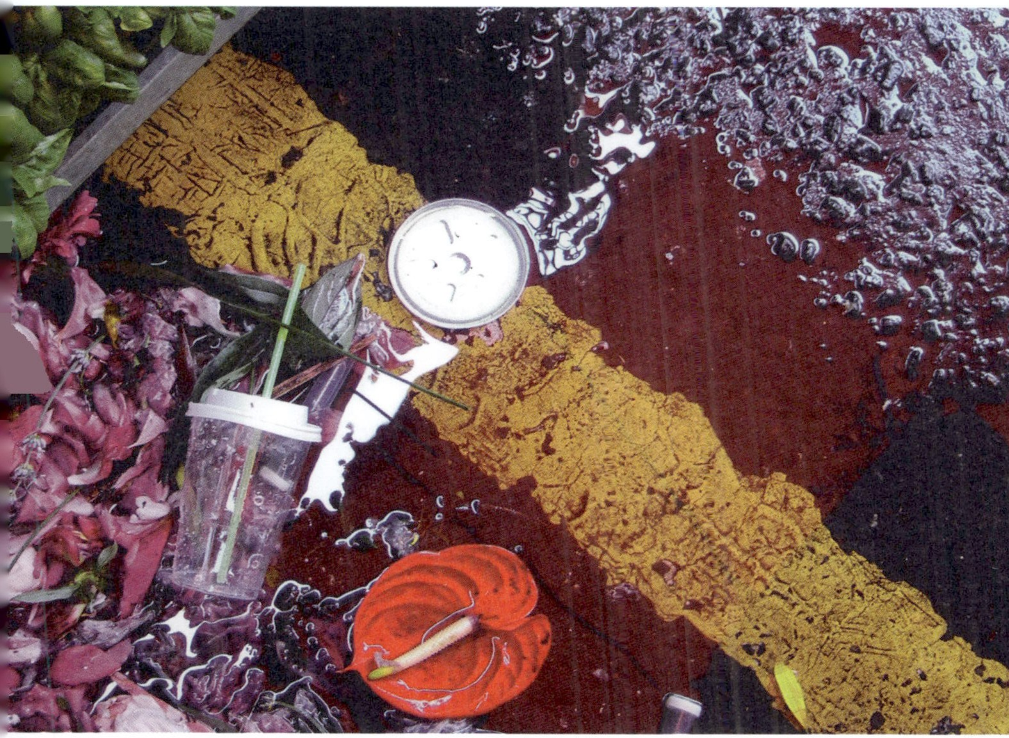

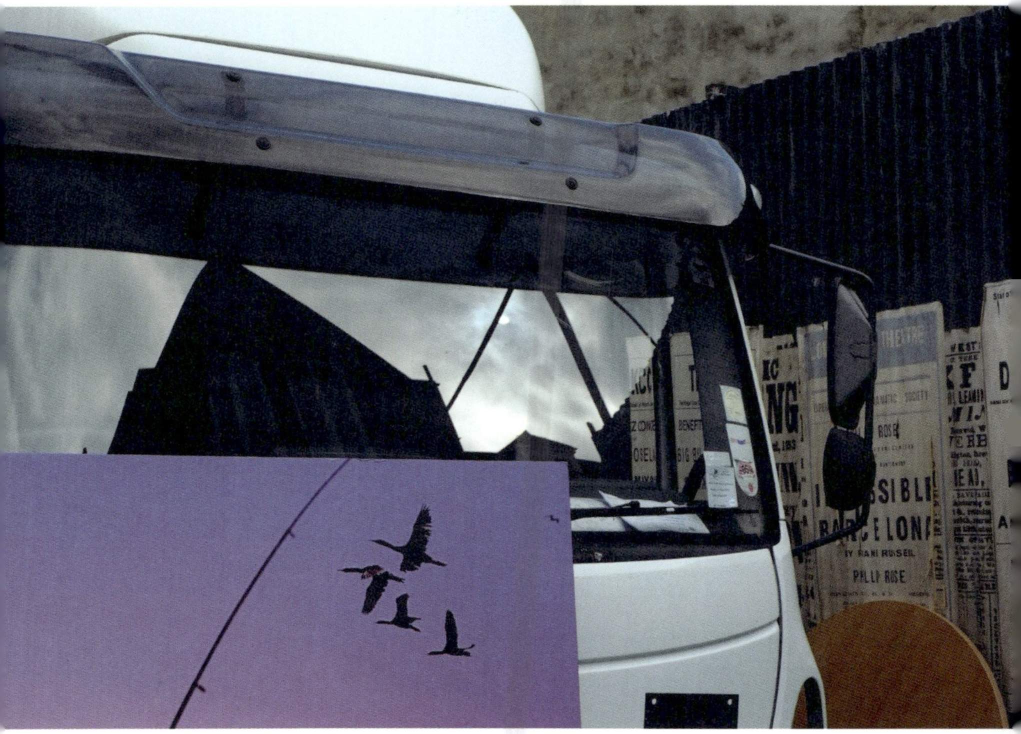
THEATRE
BENEFIT

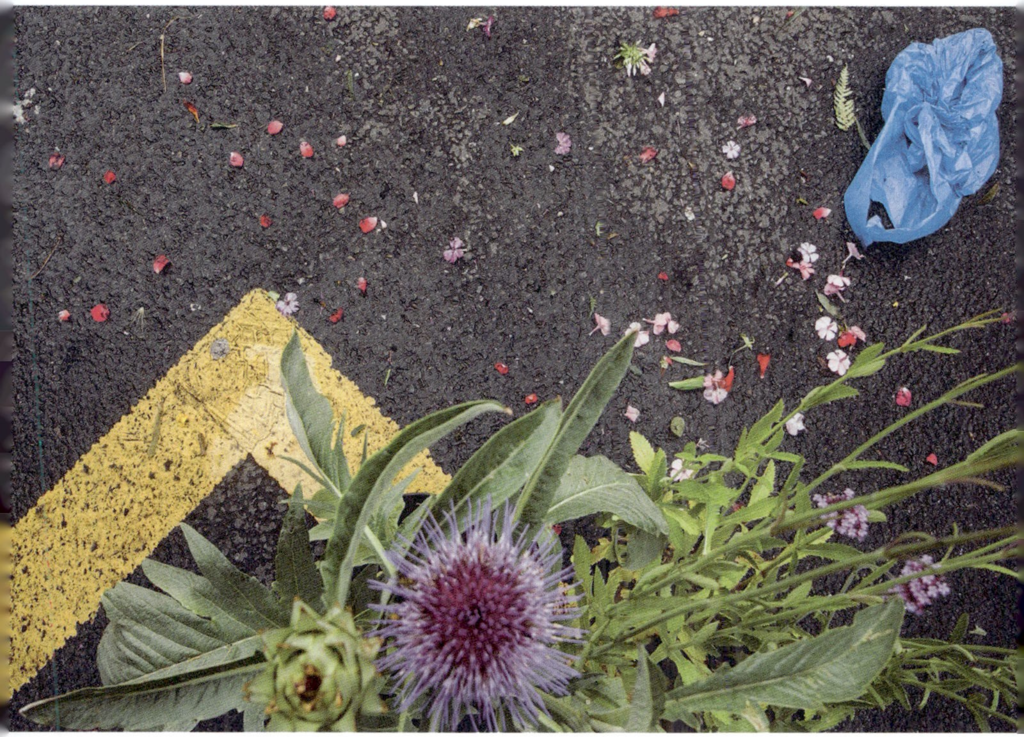

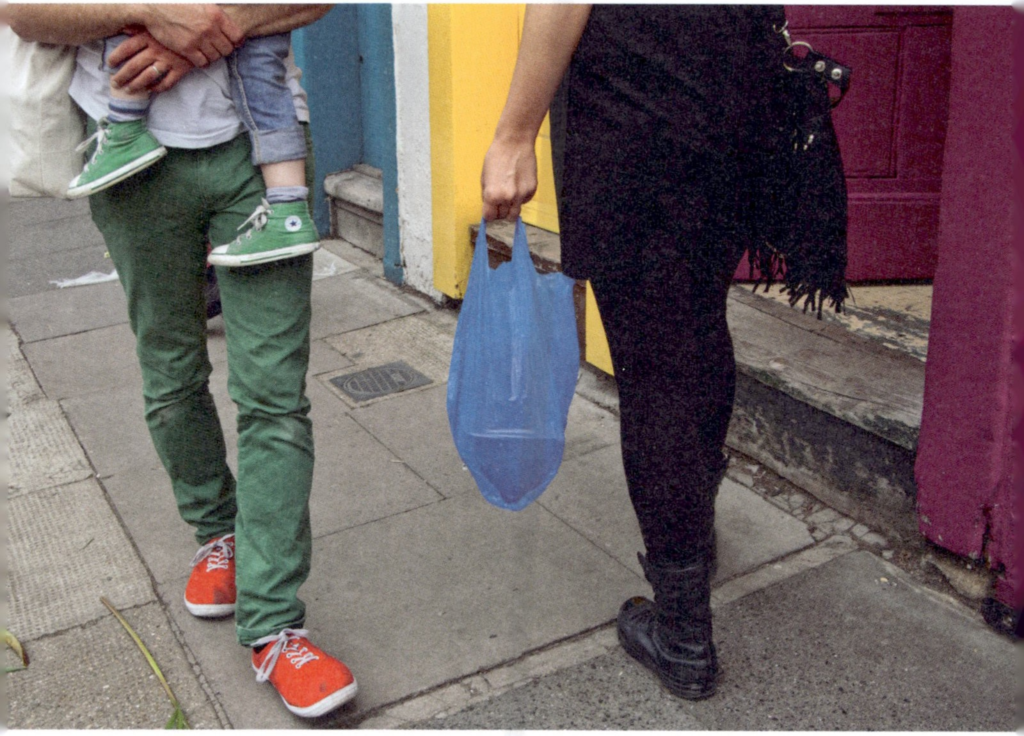

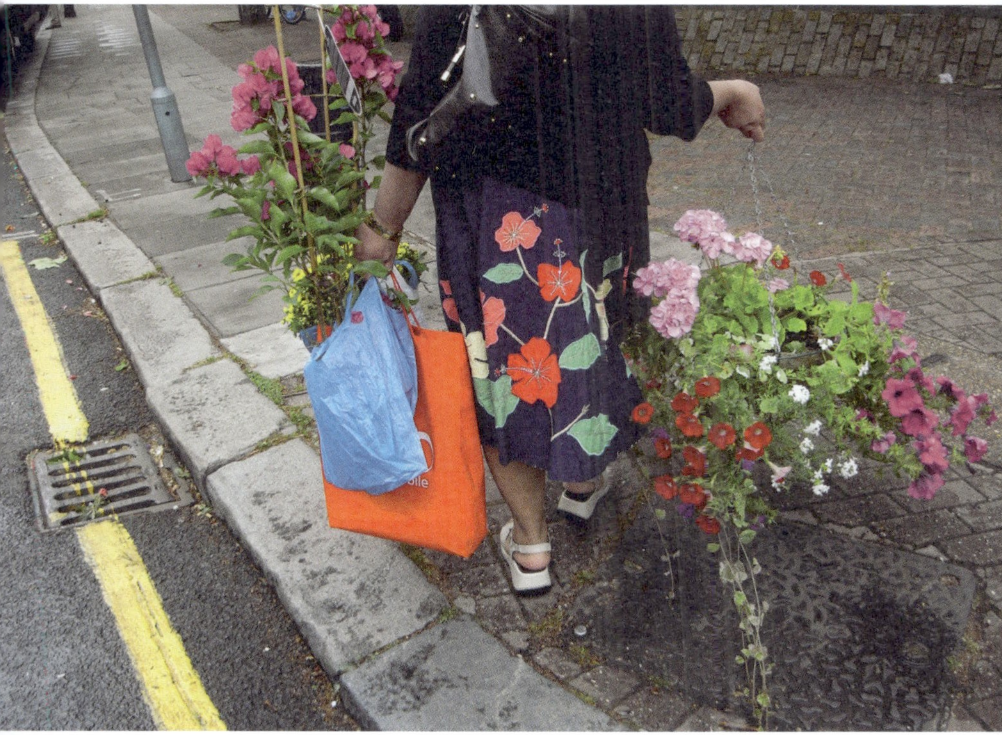

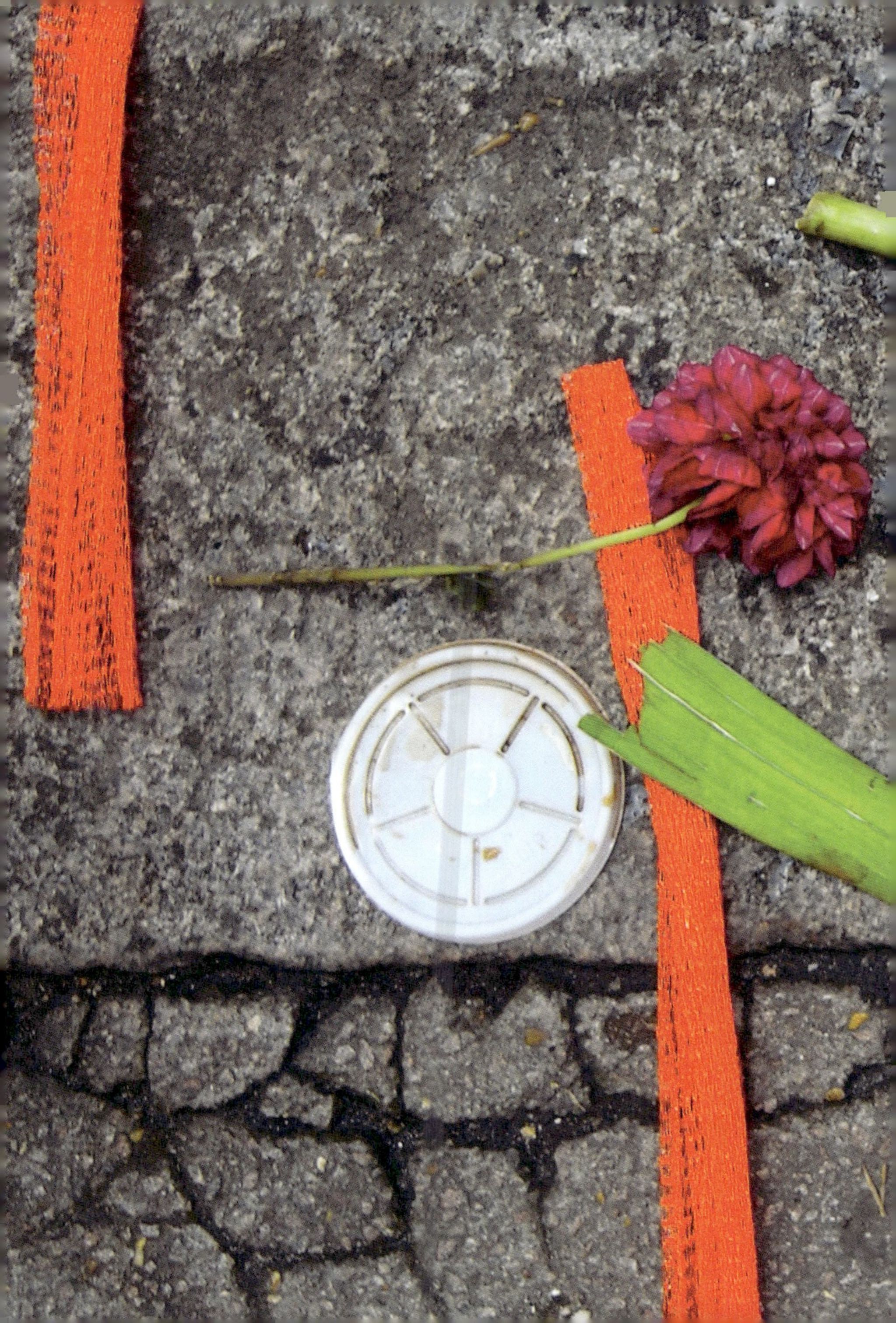

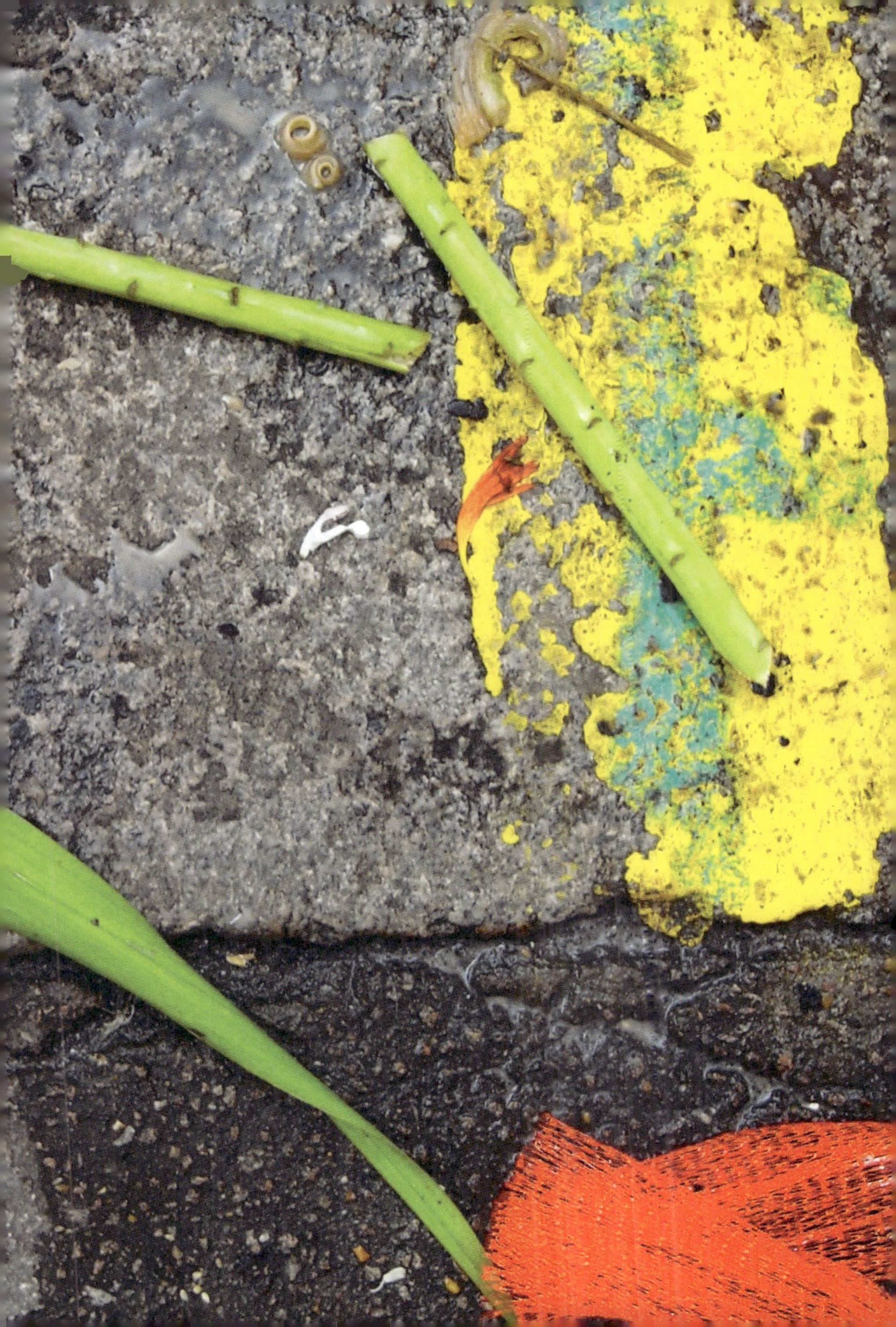

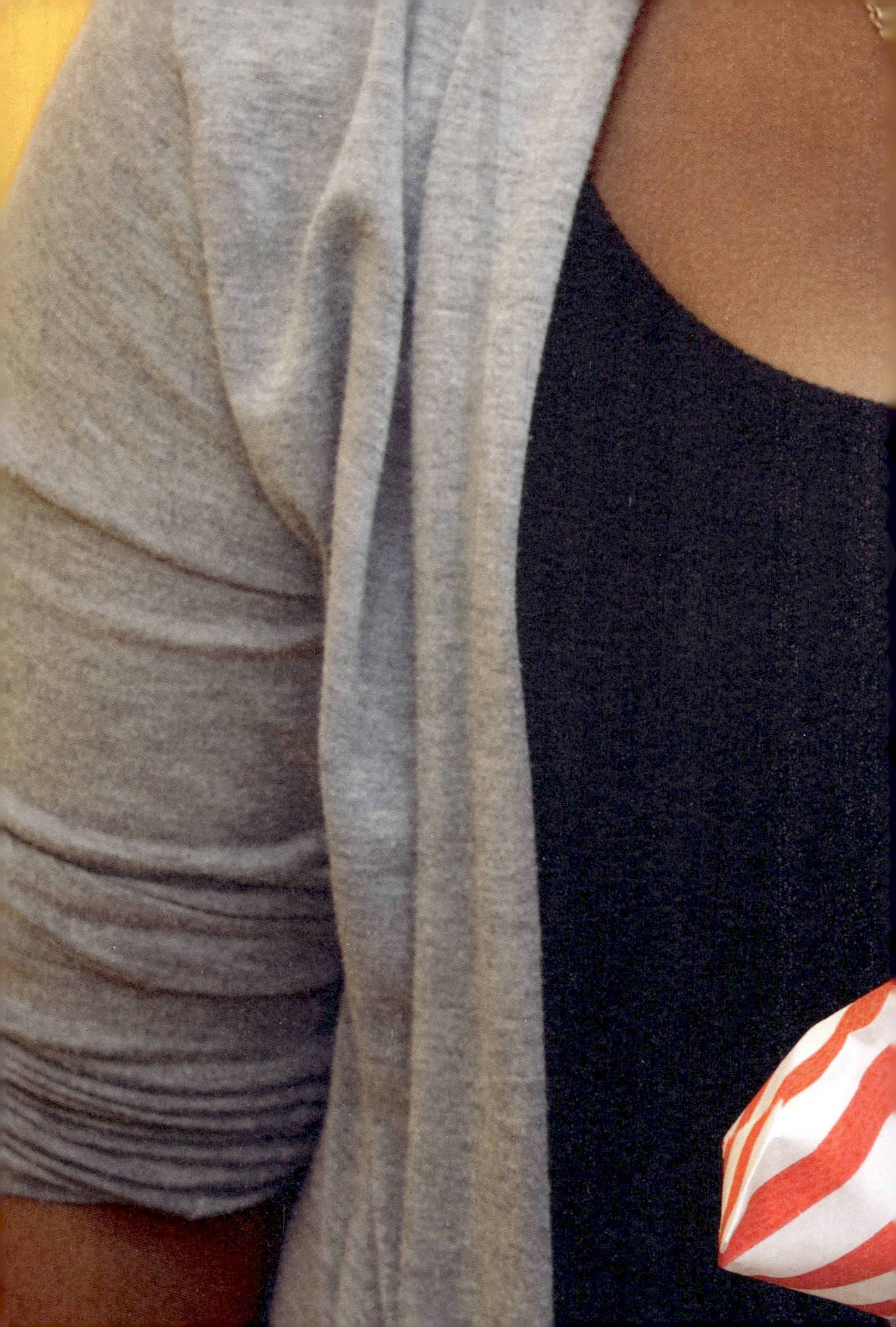

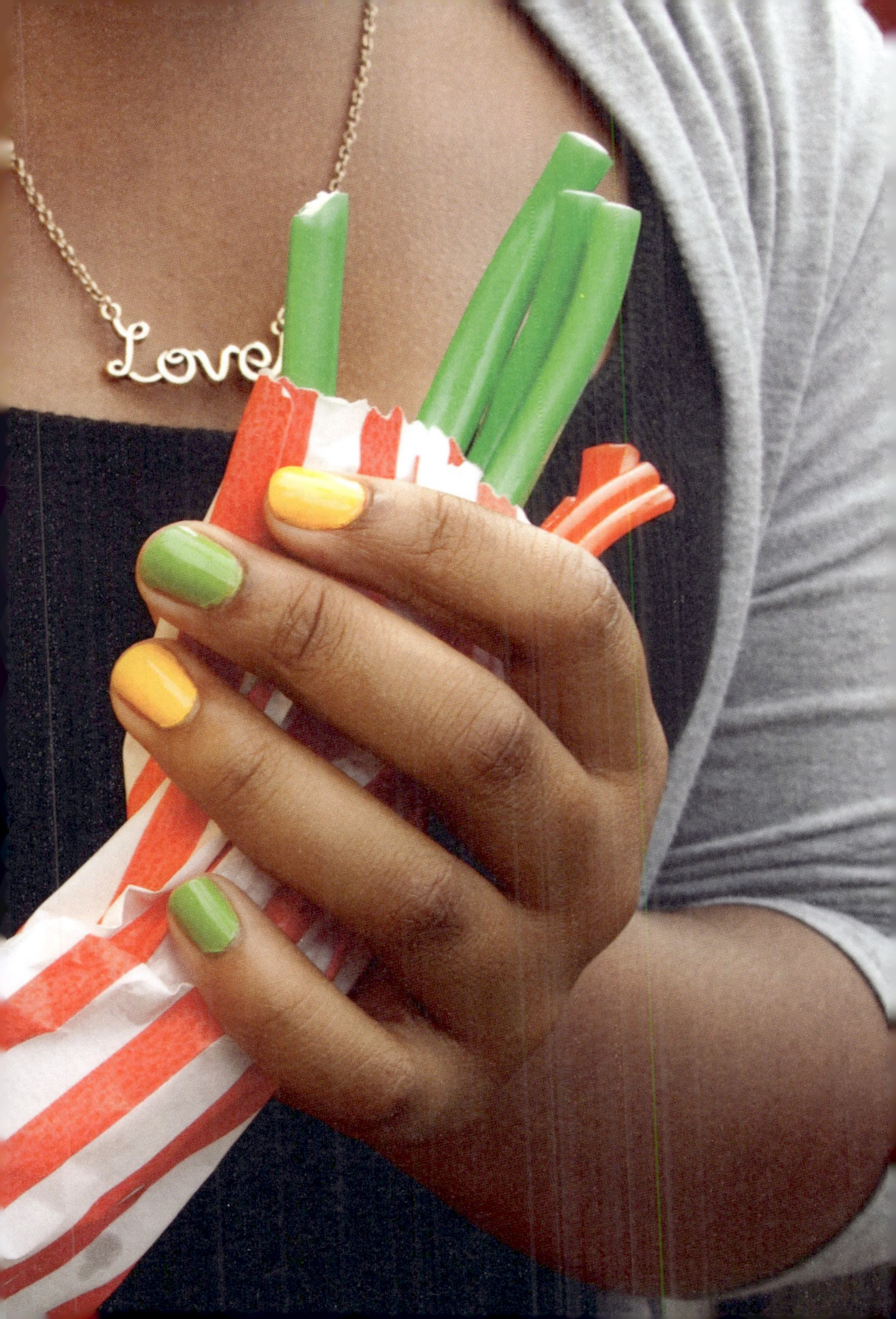
Love

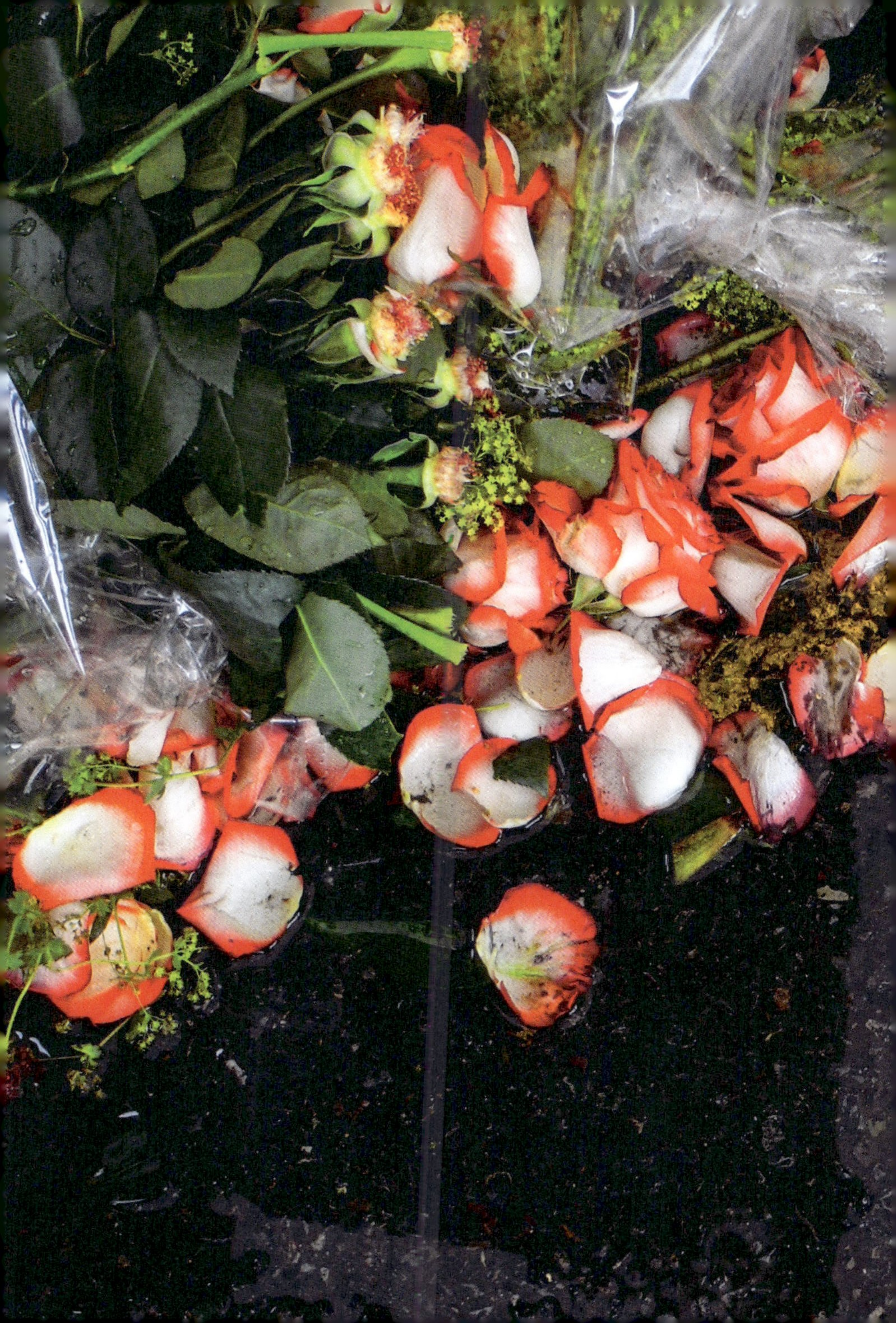

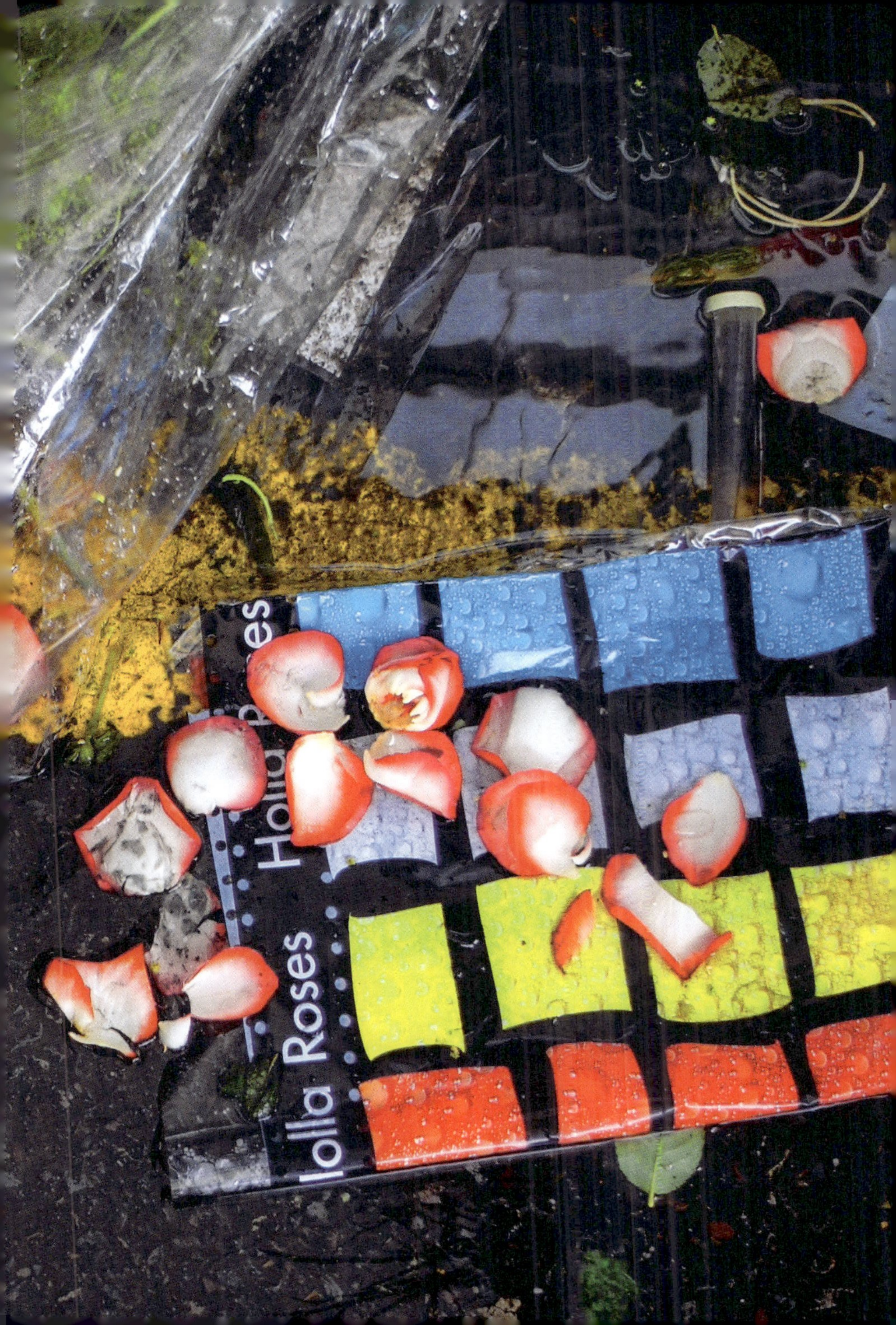
lolla Roses

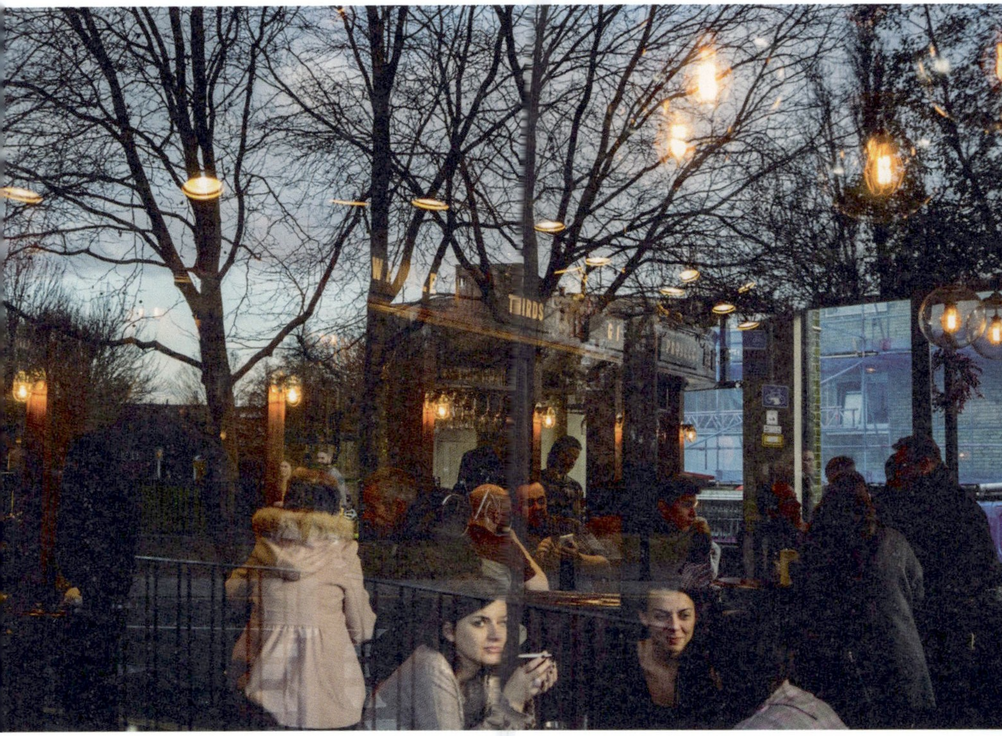

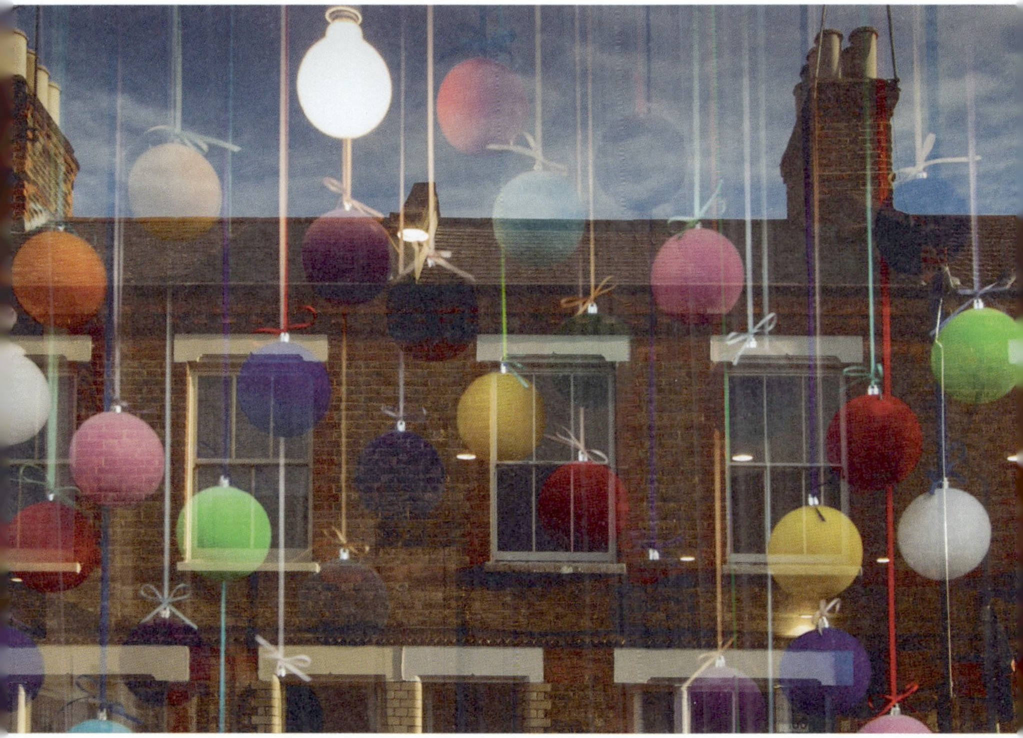

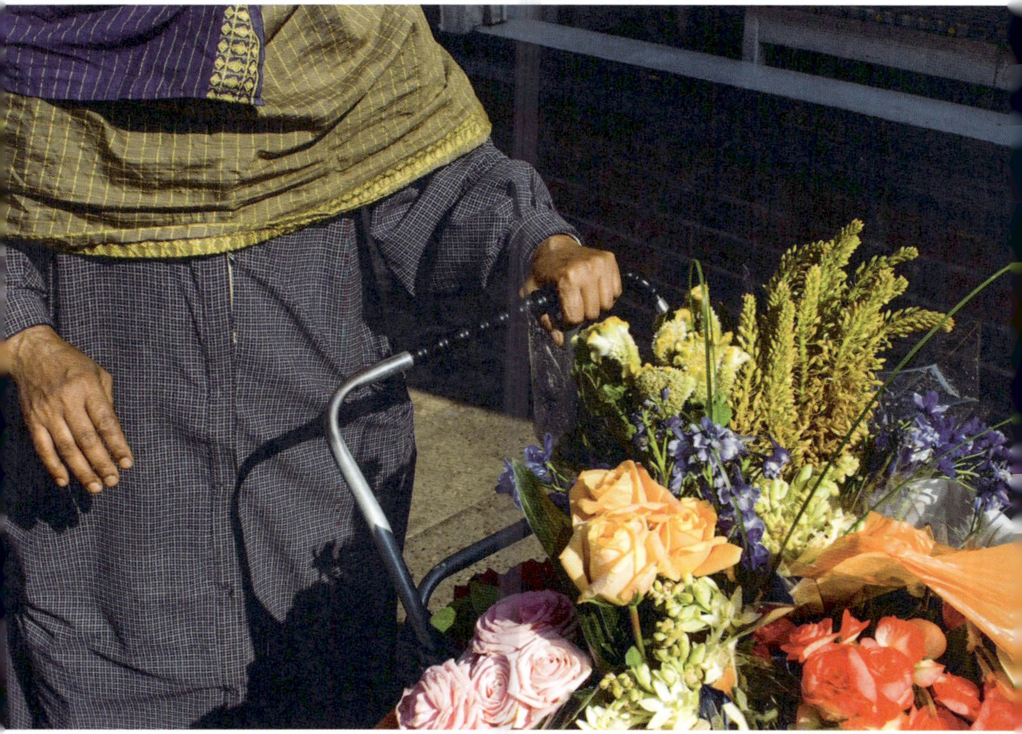

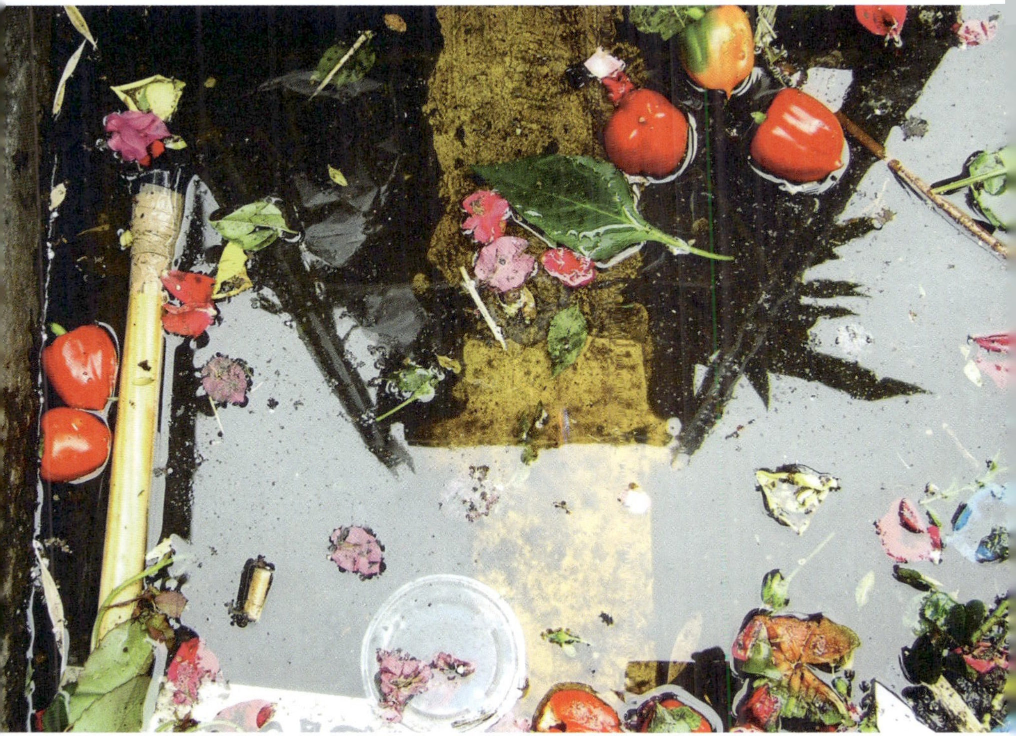

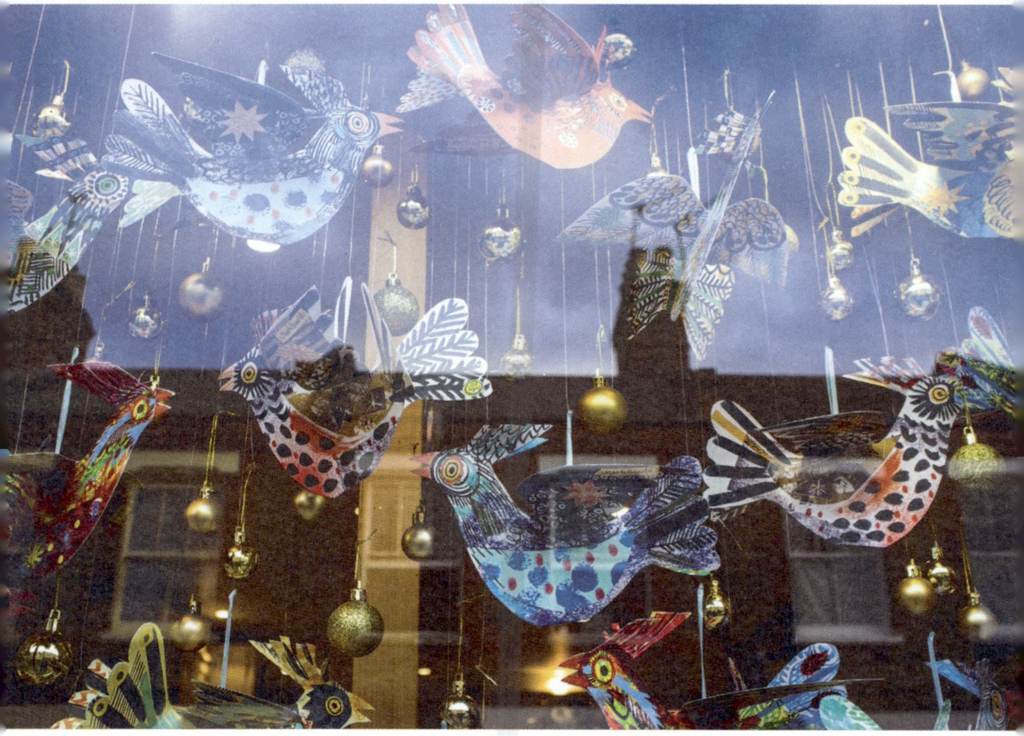

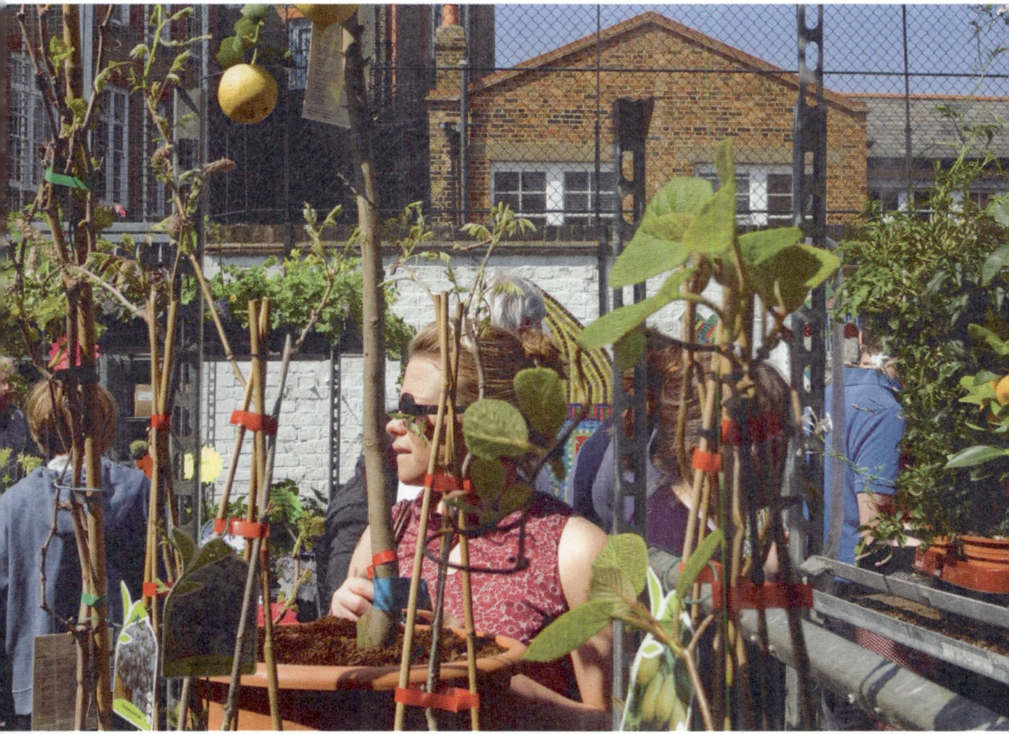

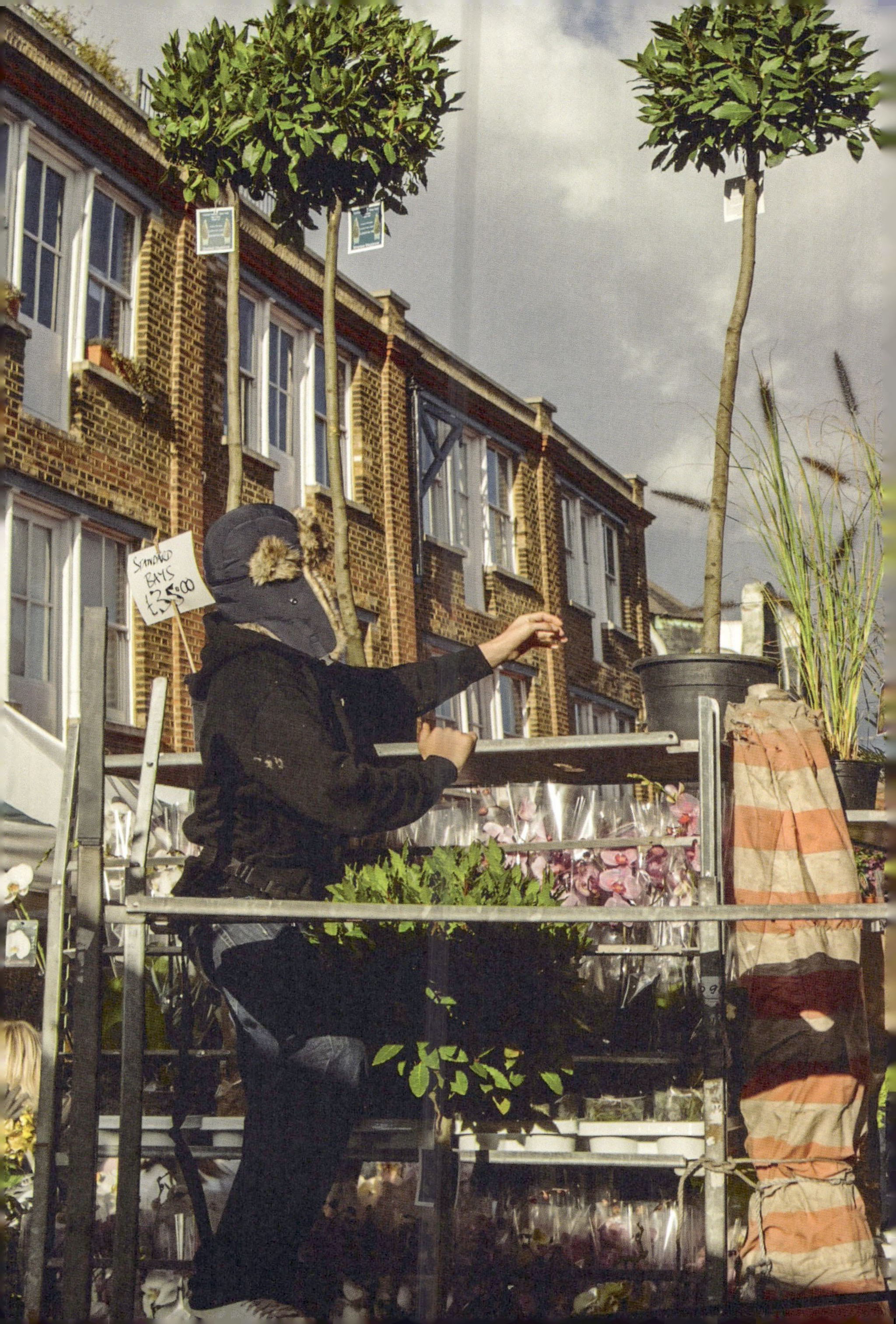
STANDARD
BAYS
£35.00

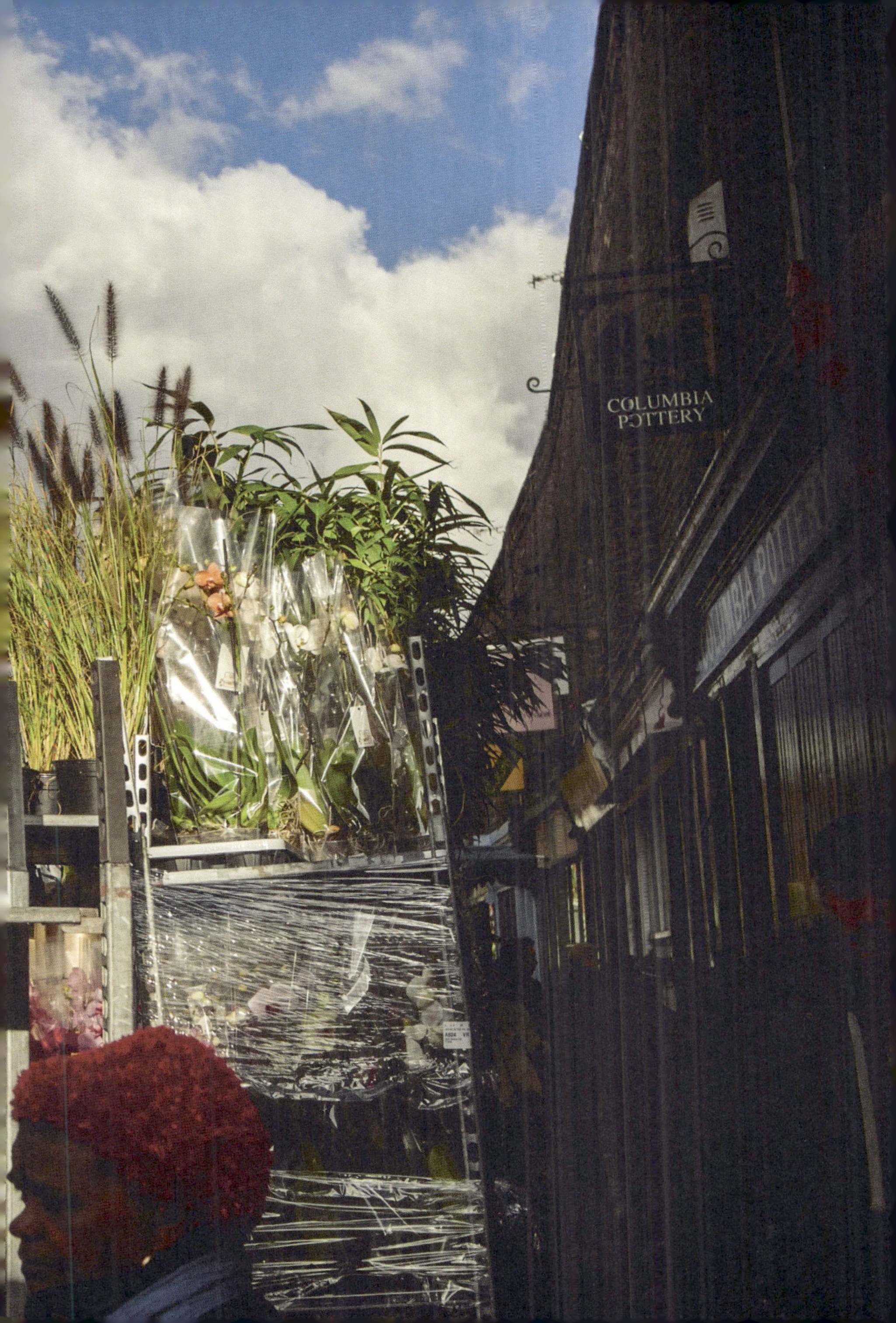
COLUMBIA
POTTERY

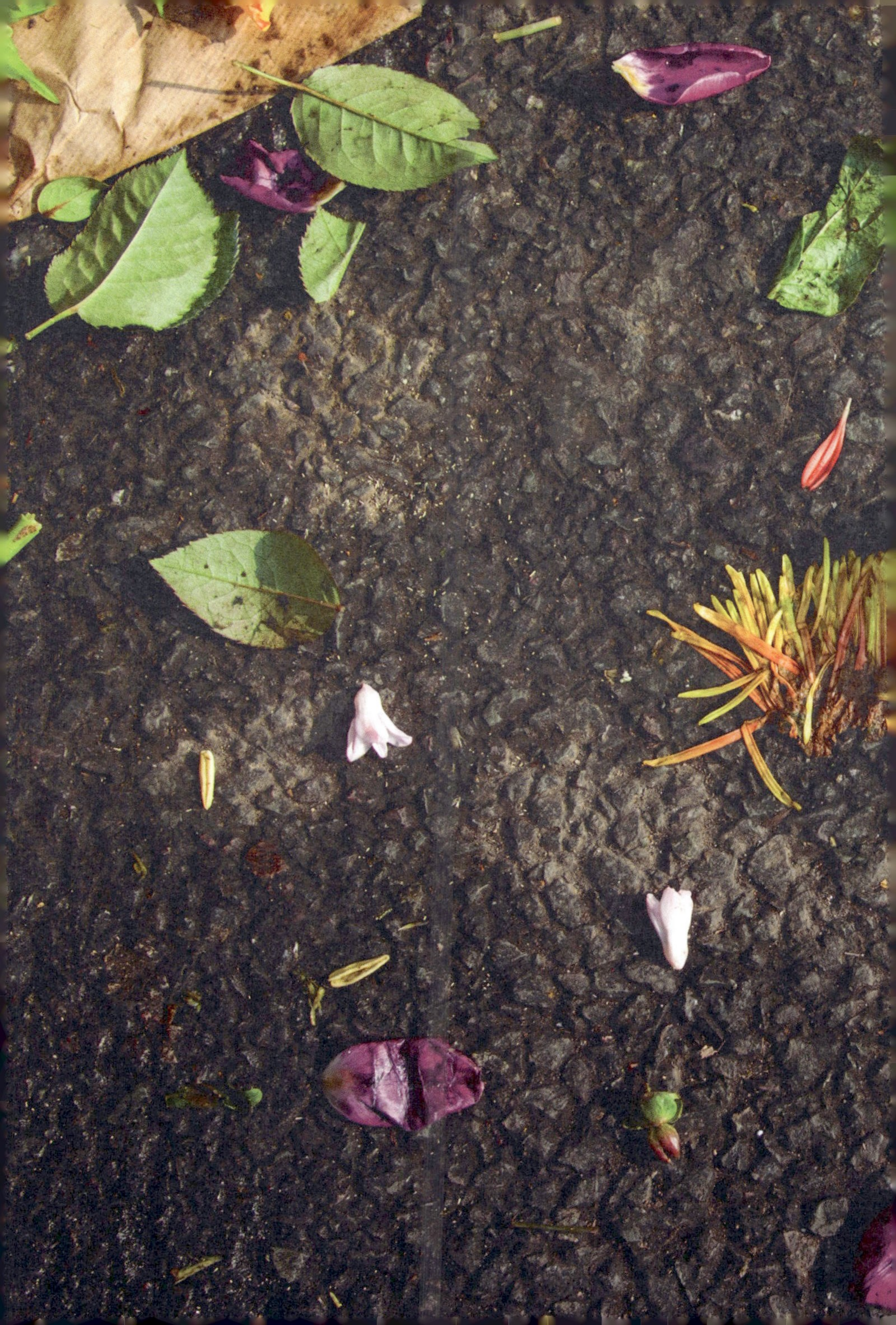

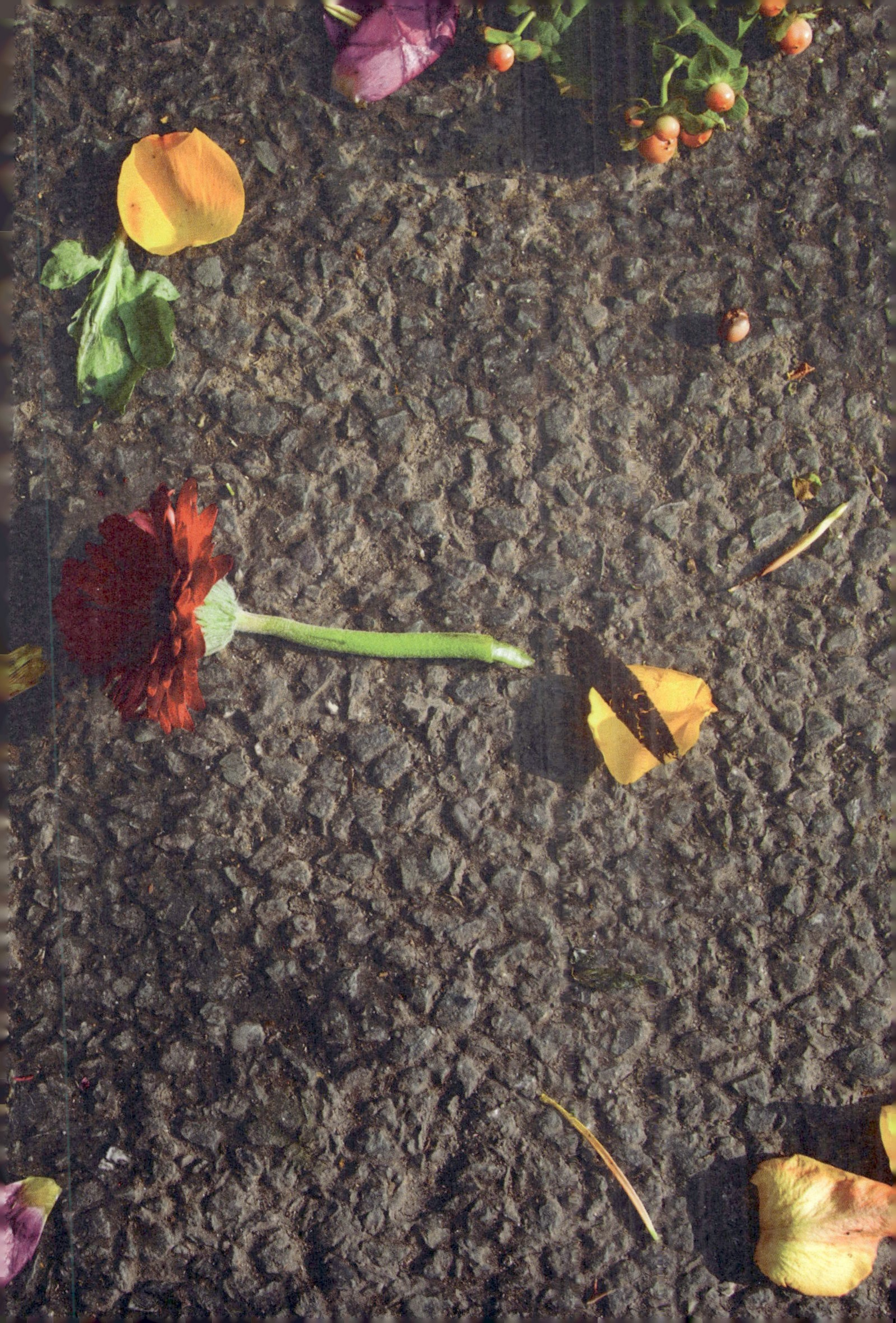

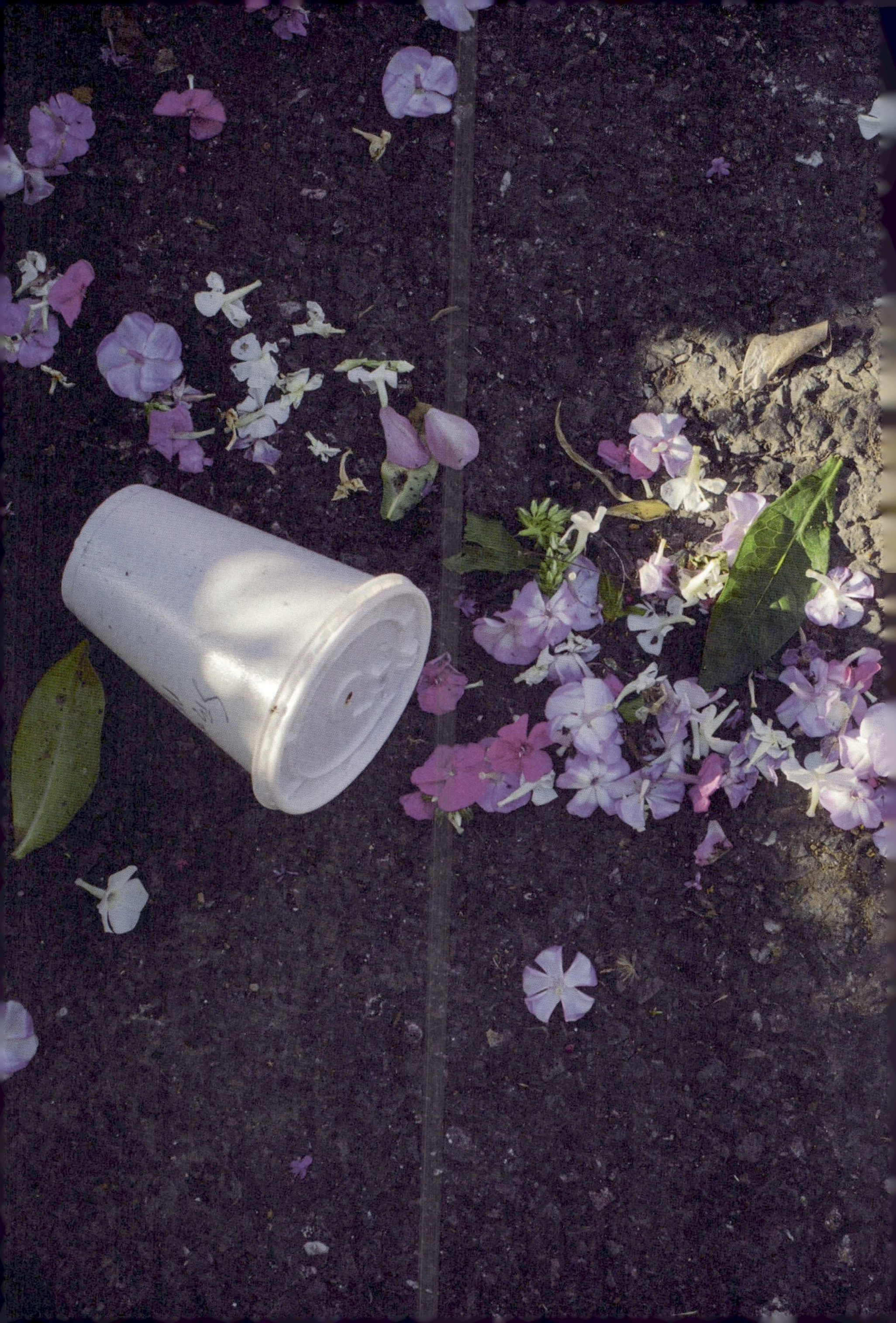

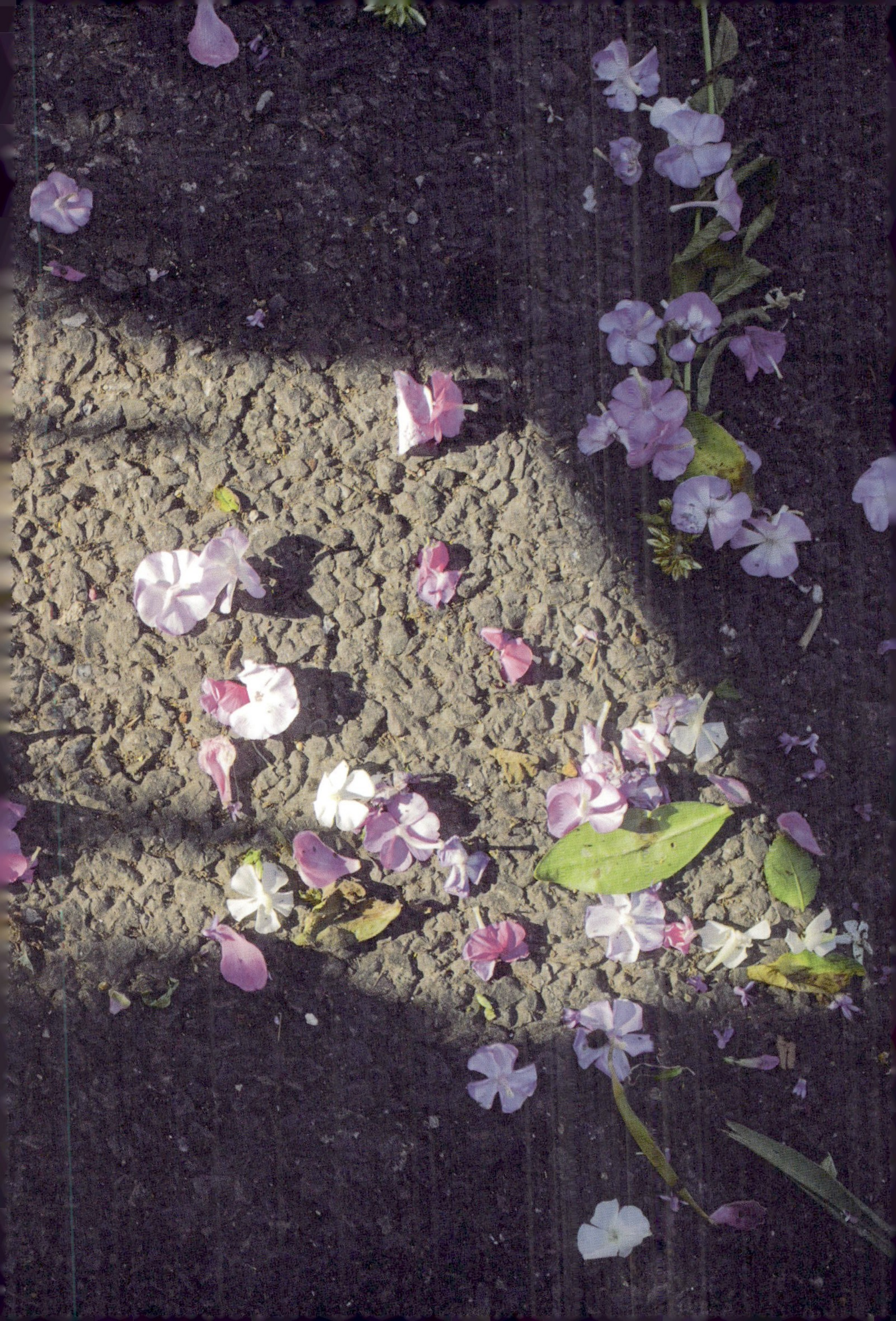

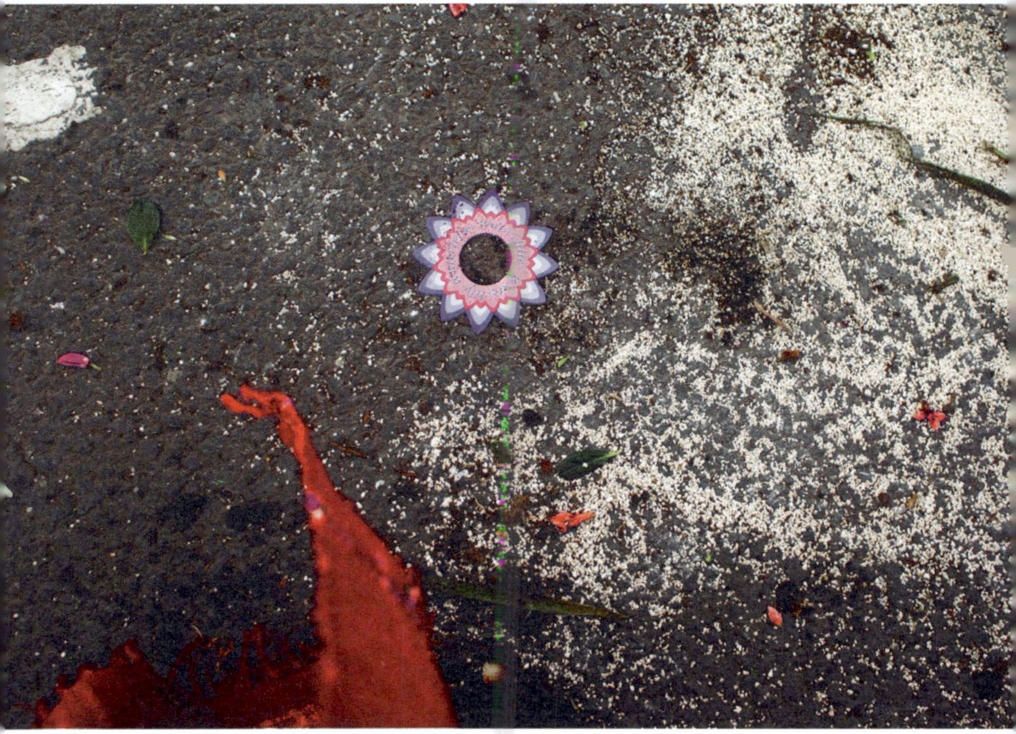

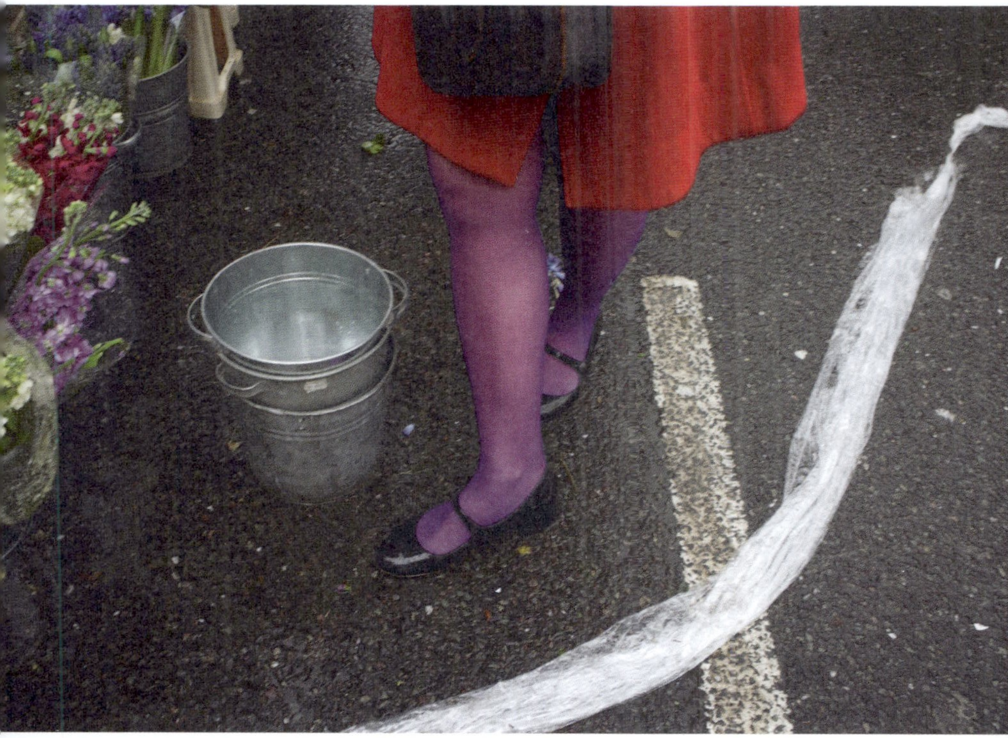

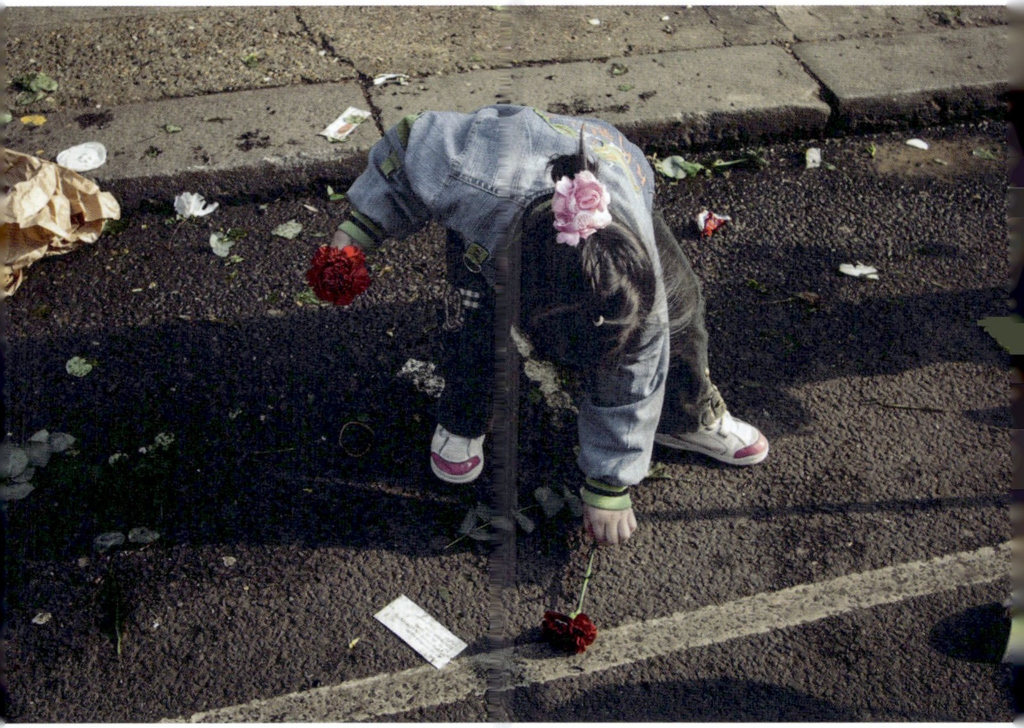

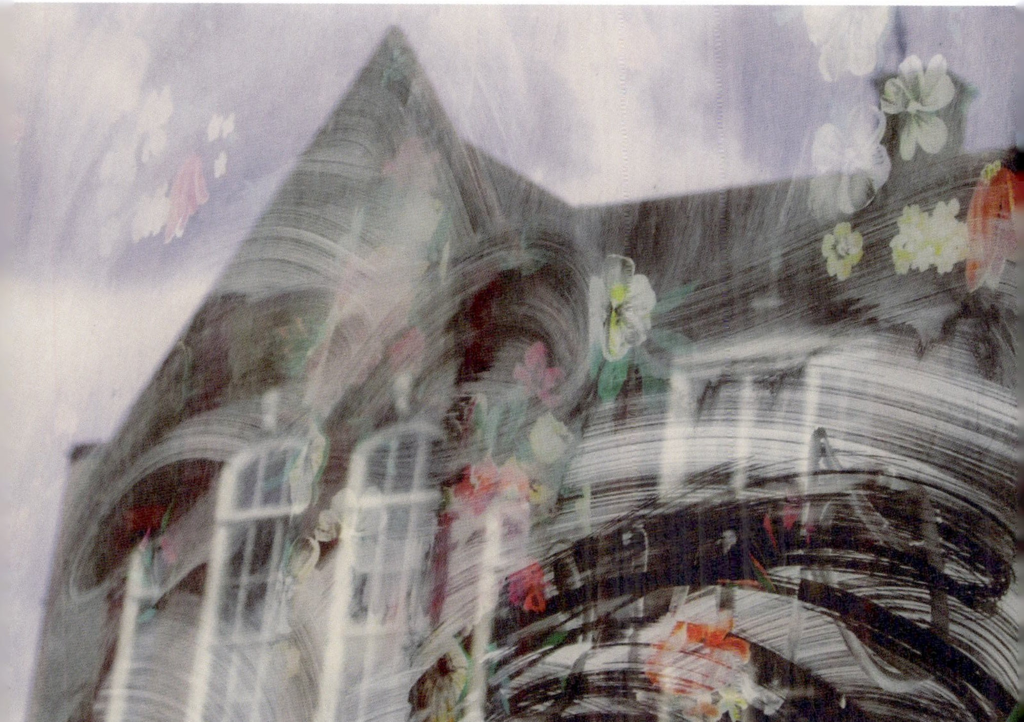

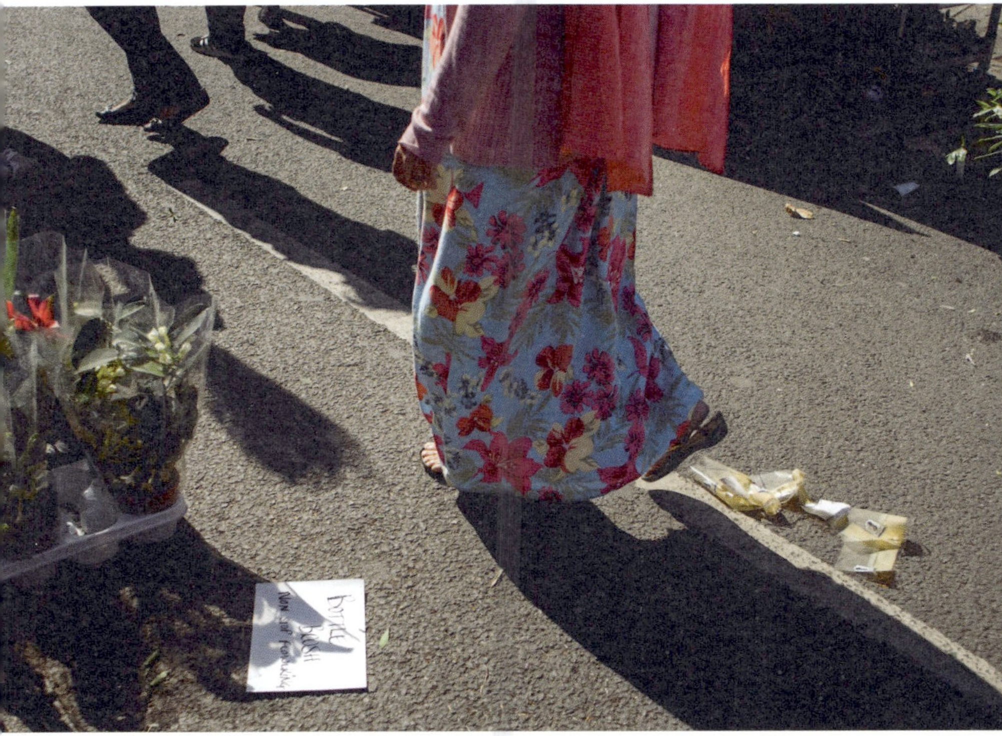

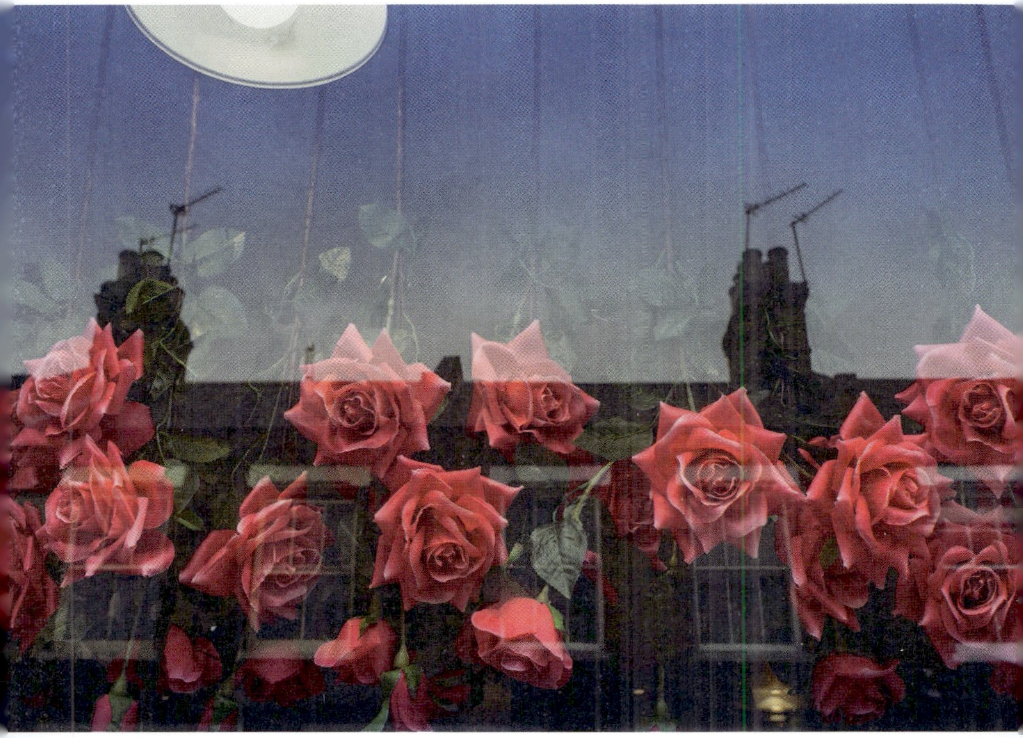

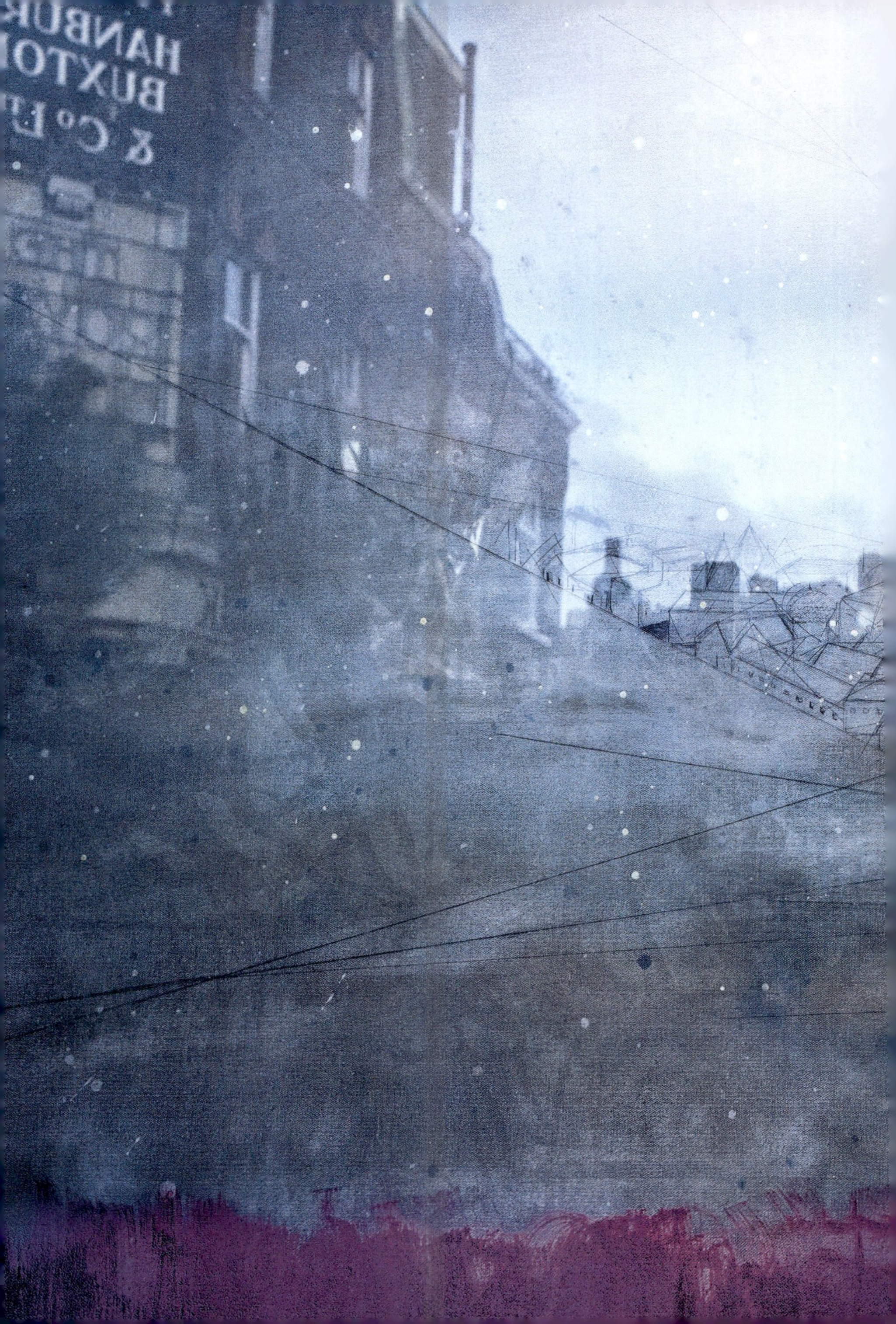
HANBUR
BUXTO
B
& Co

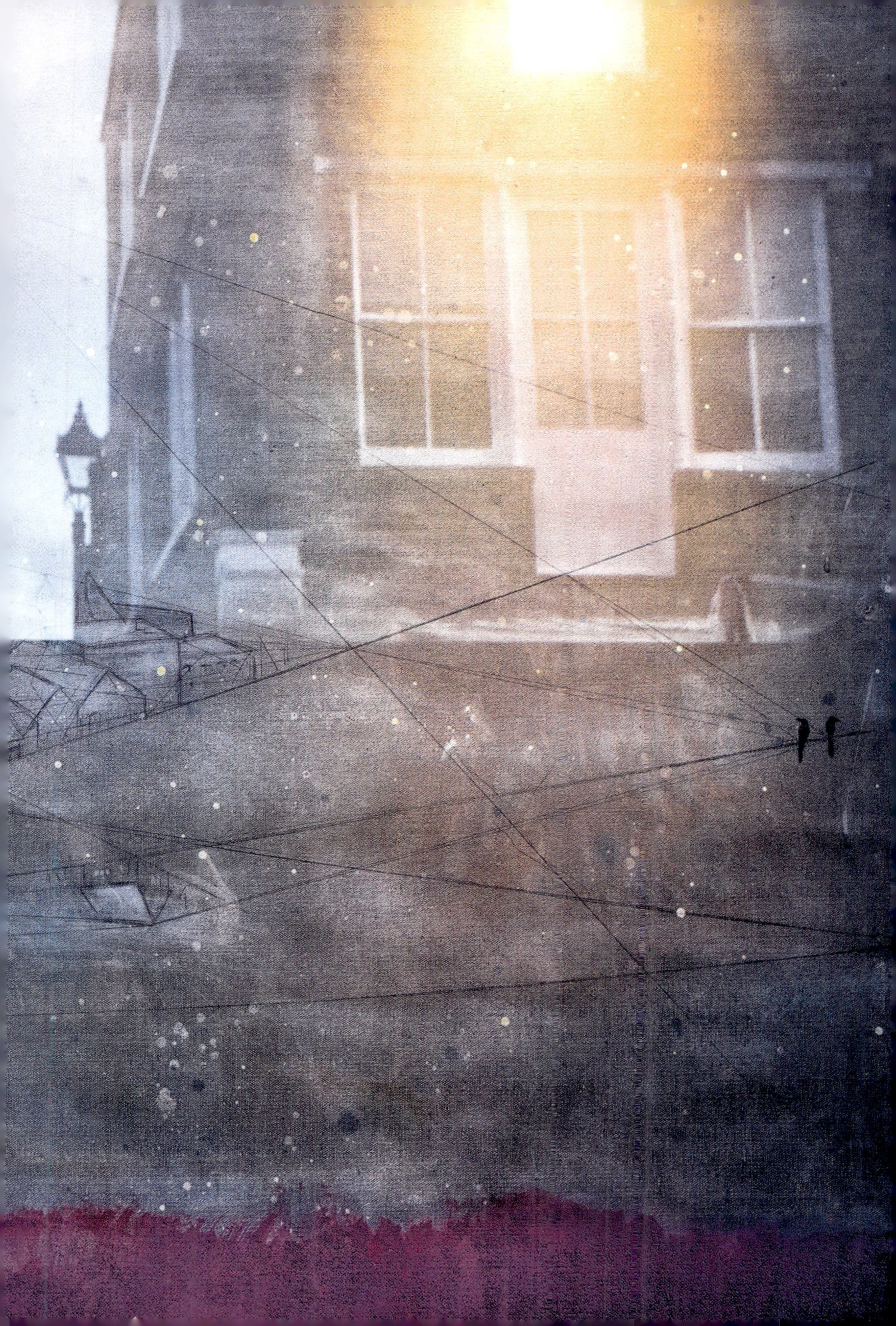

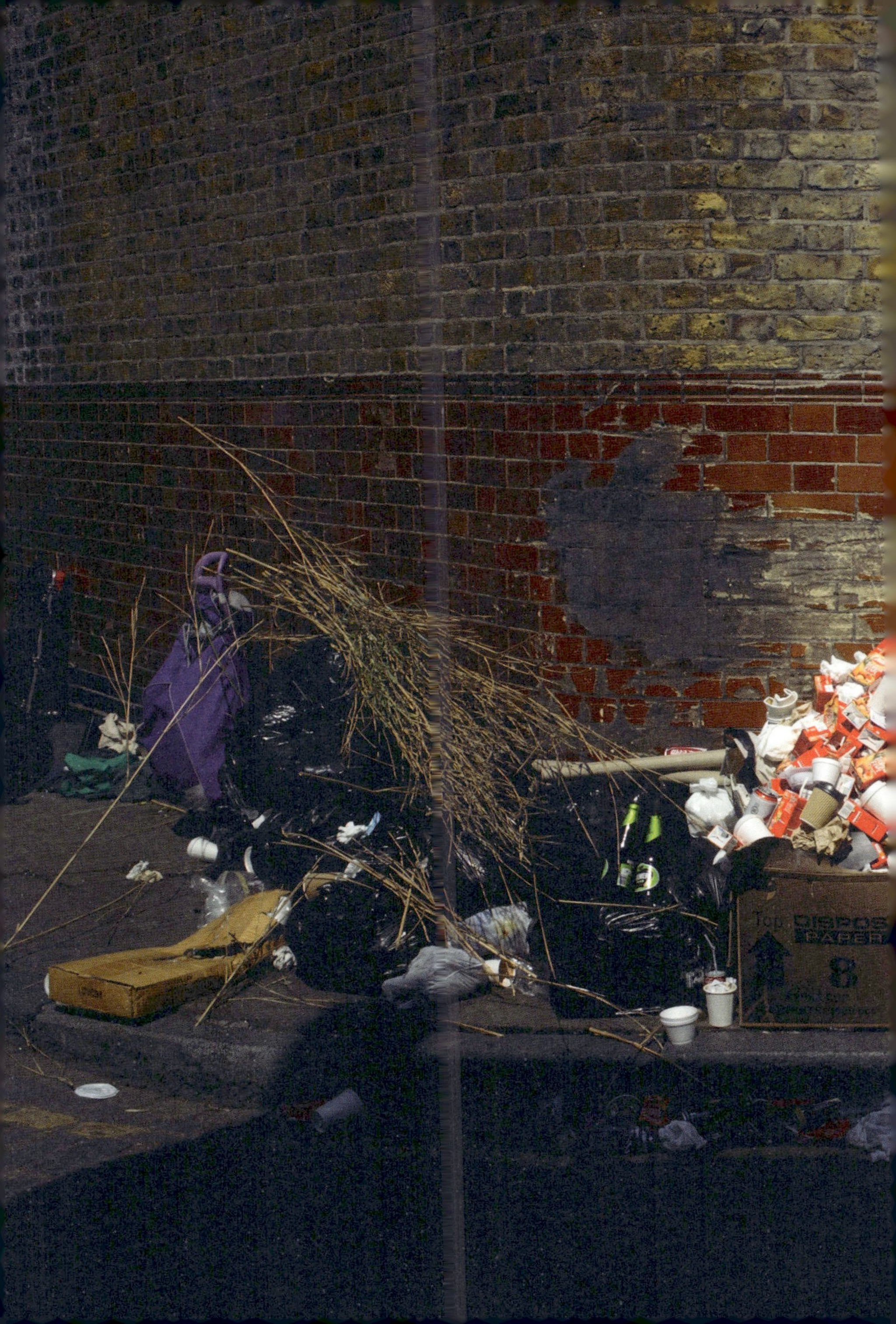
Top
DISPOS
PAPER
8

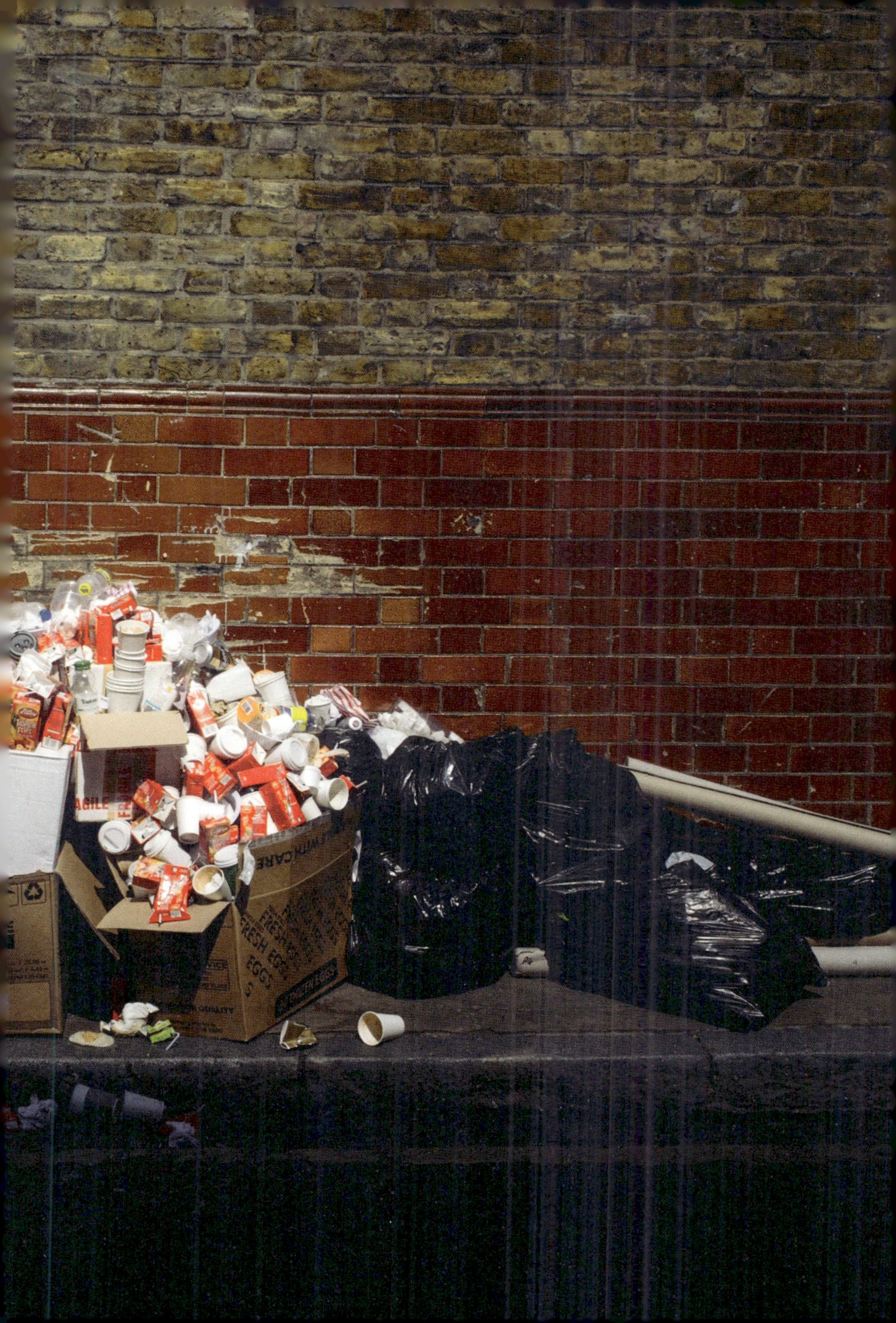

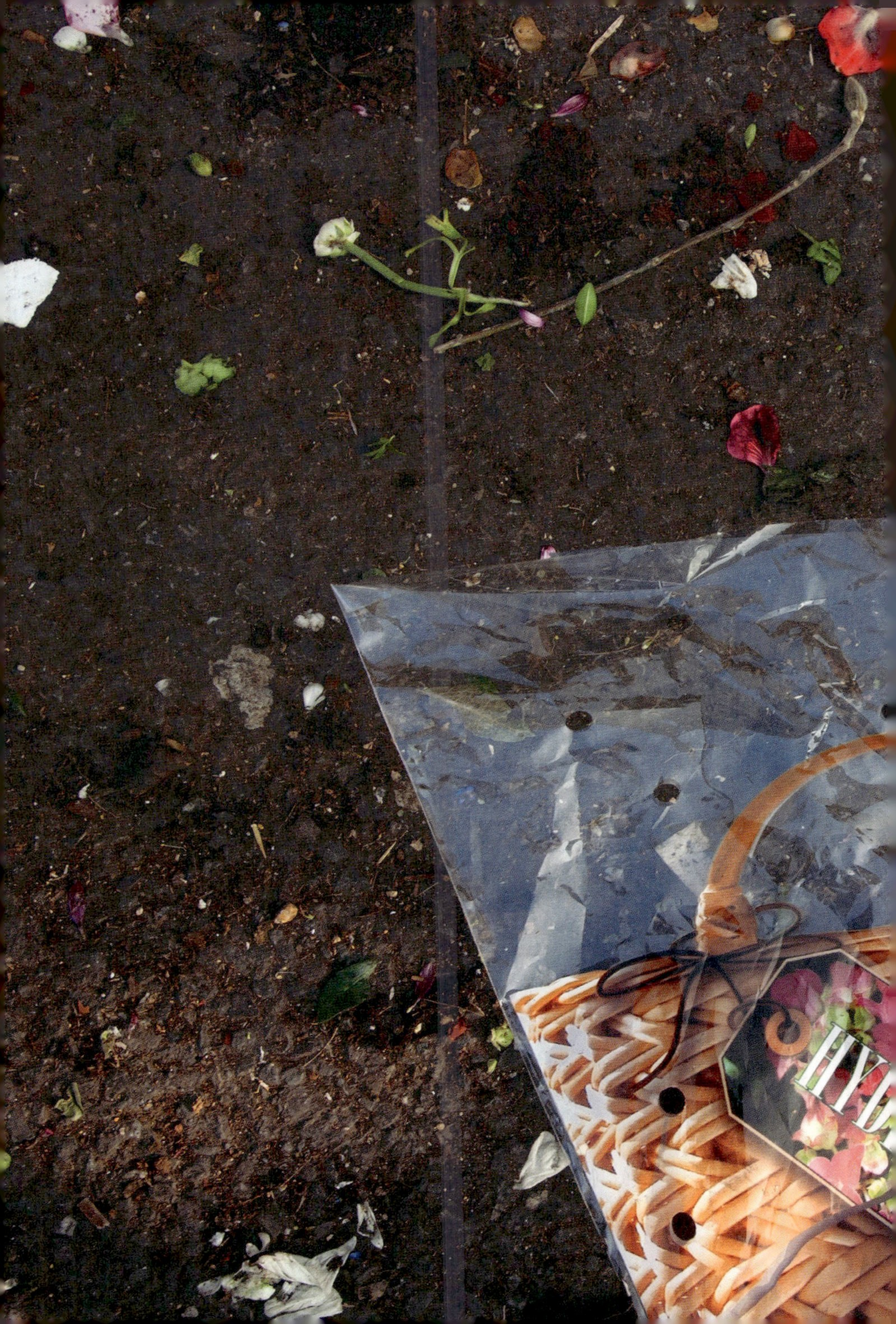

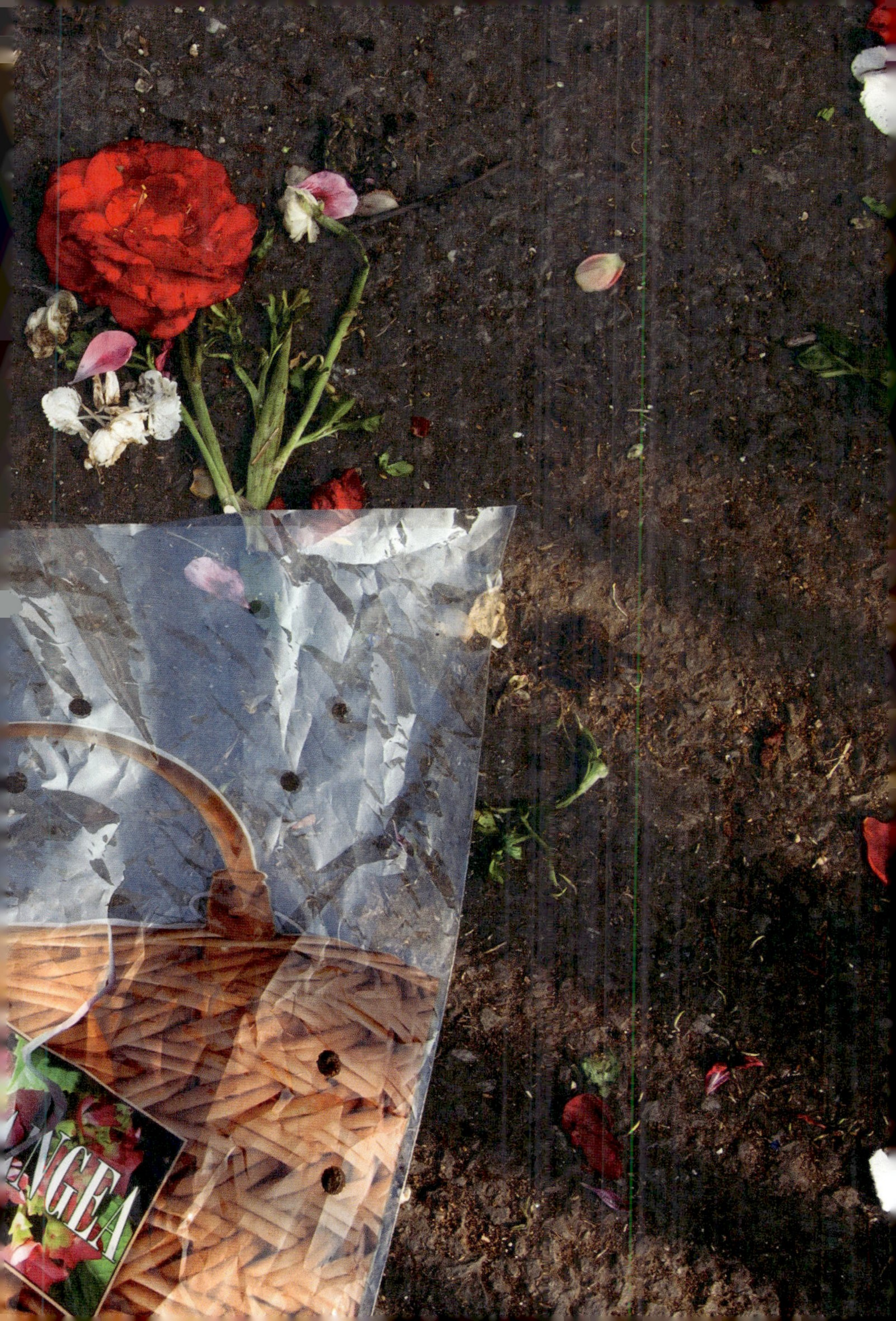

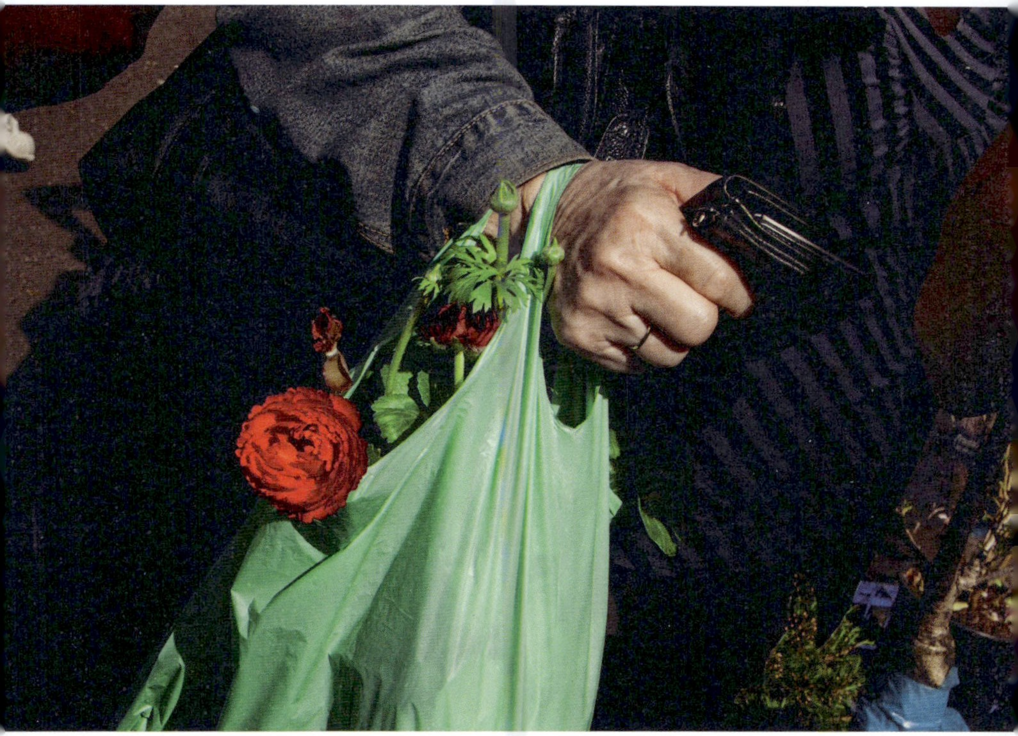

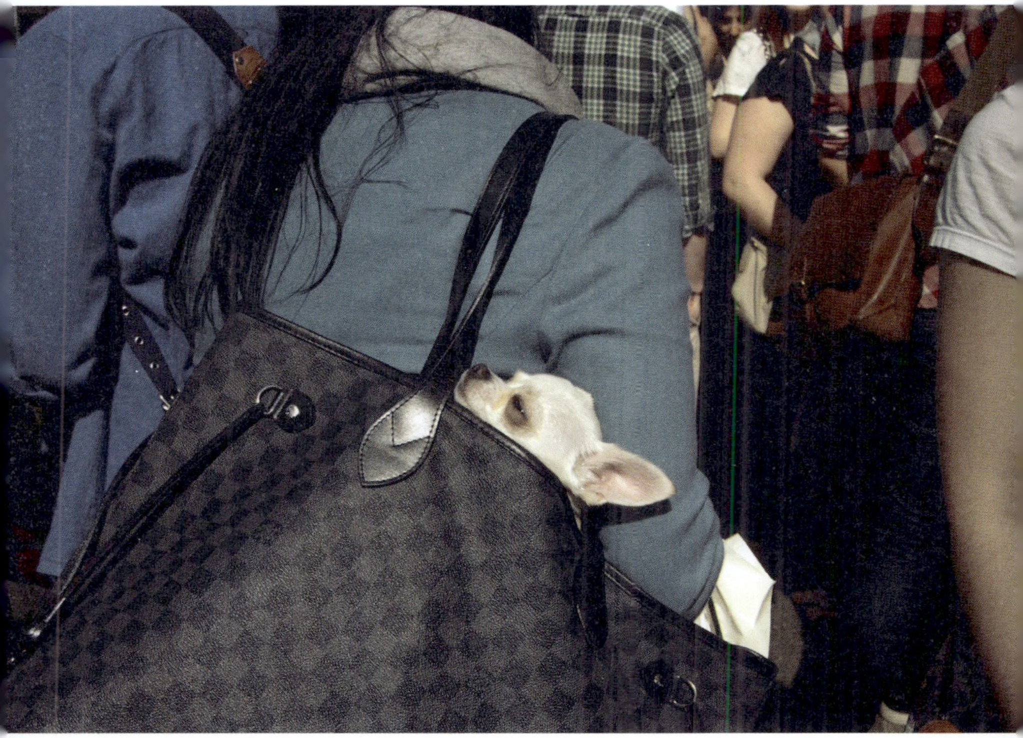

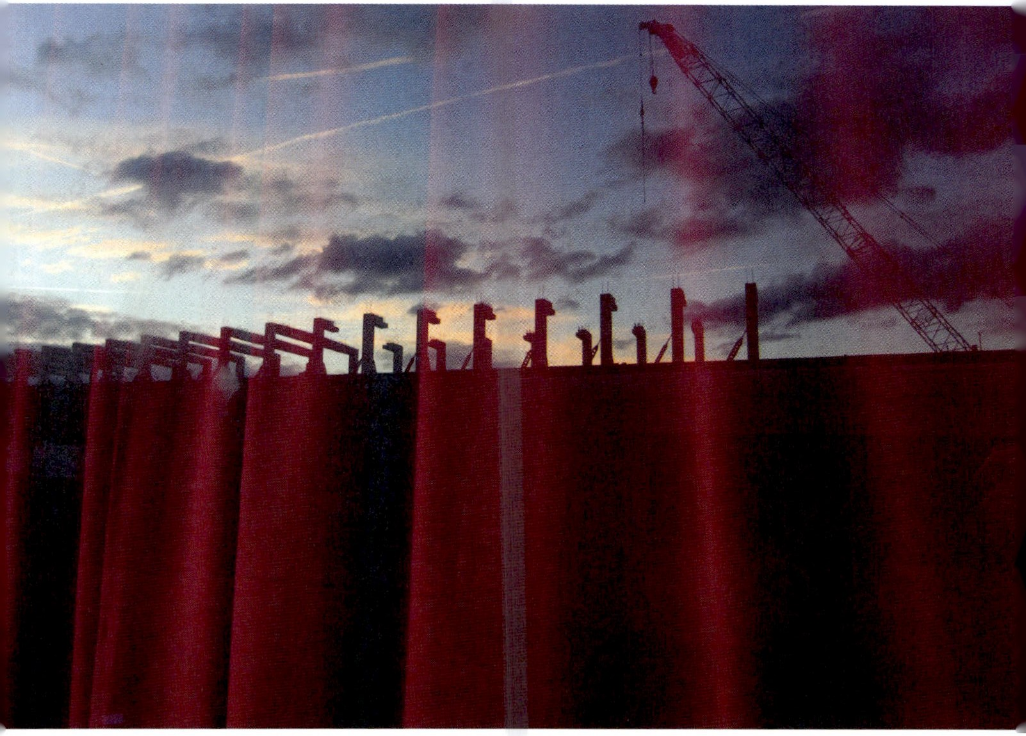

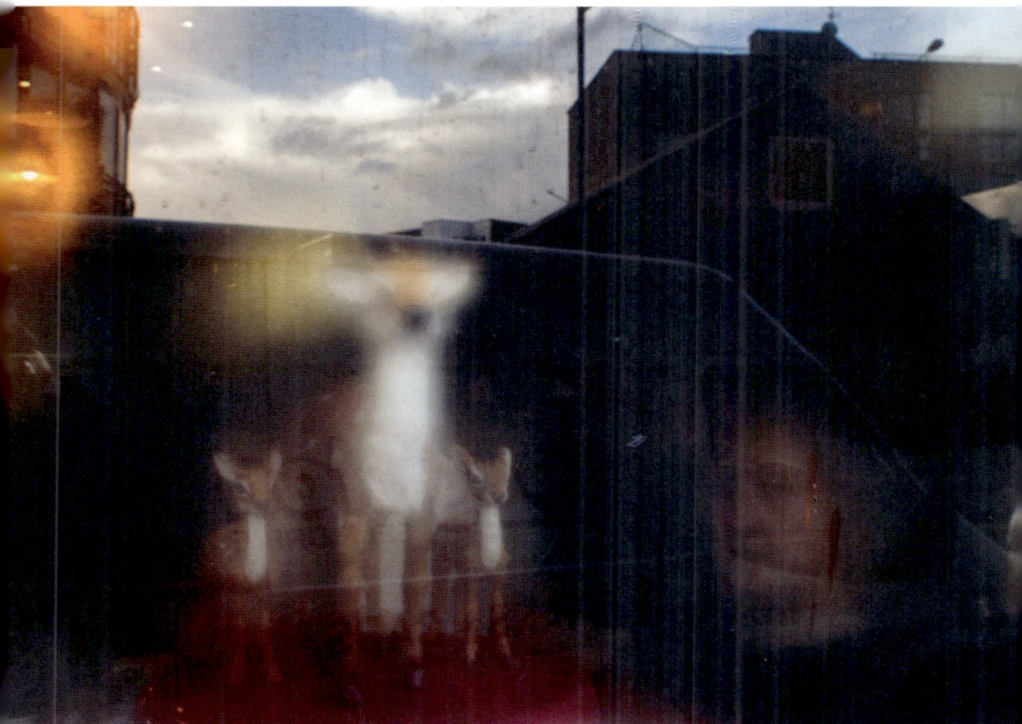

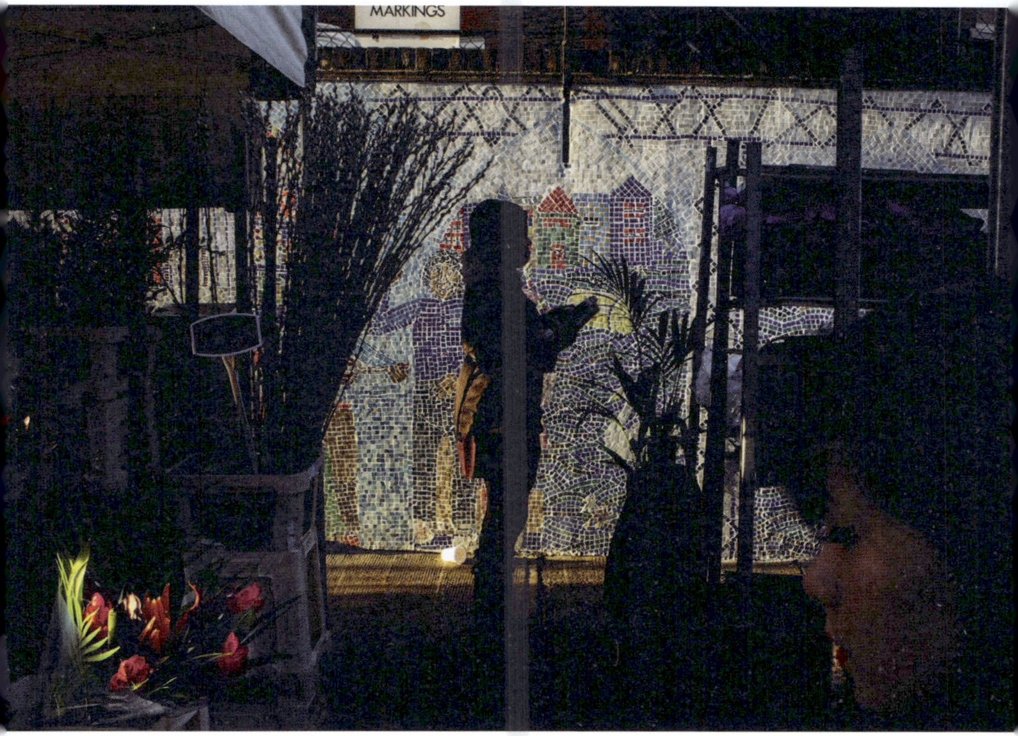
MARKINGS

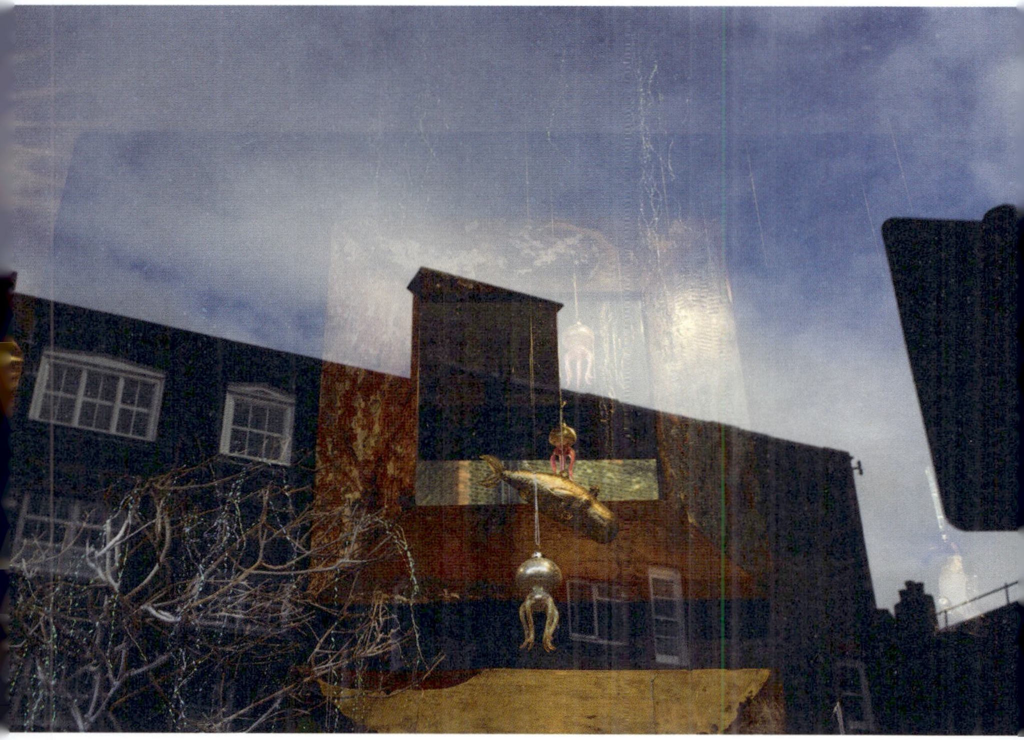

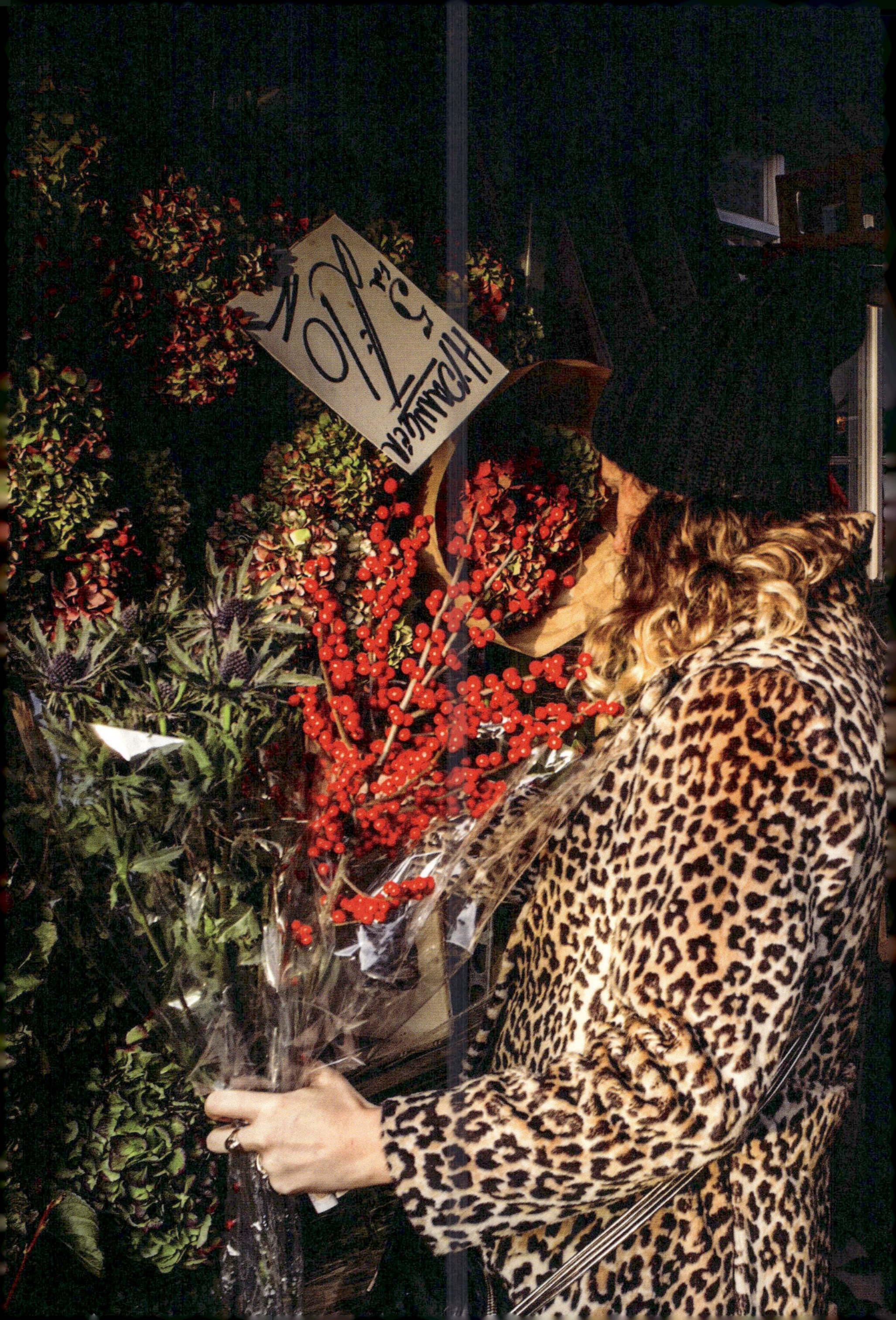

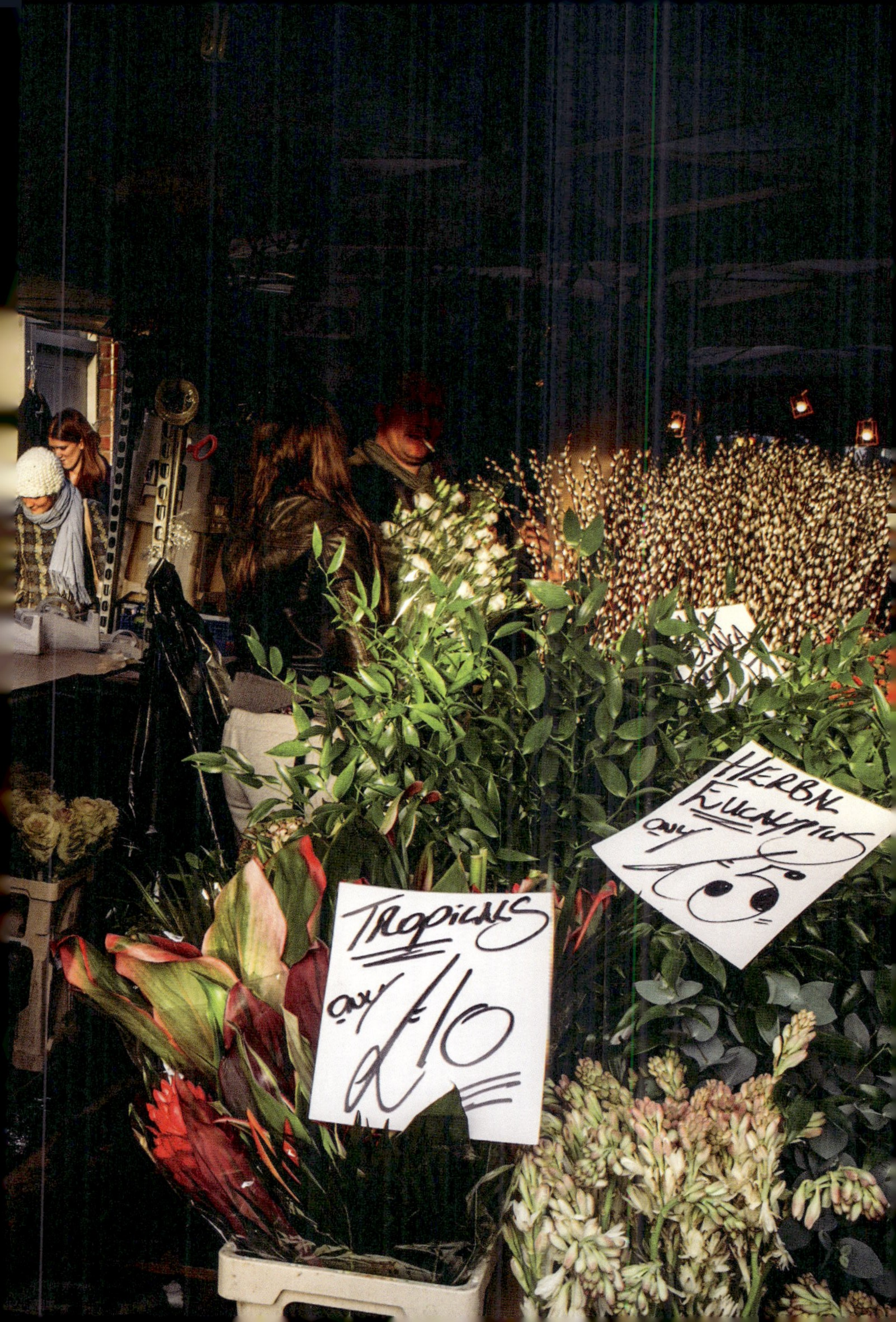
TROPICALS
ONLY £10
HERBAL
EUCALYPTUS
ONLY £10

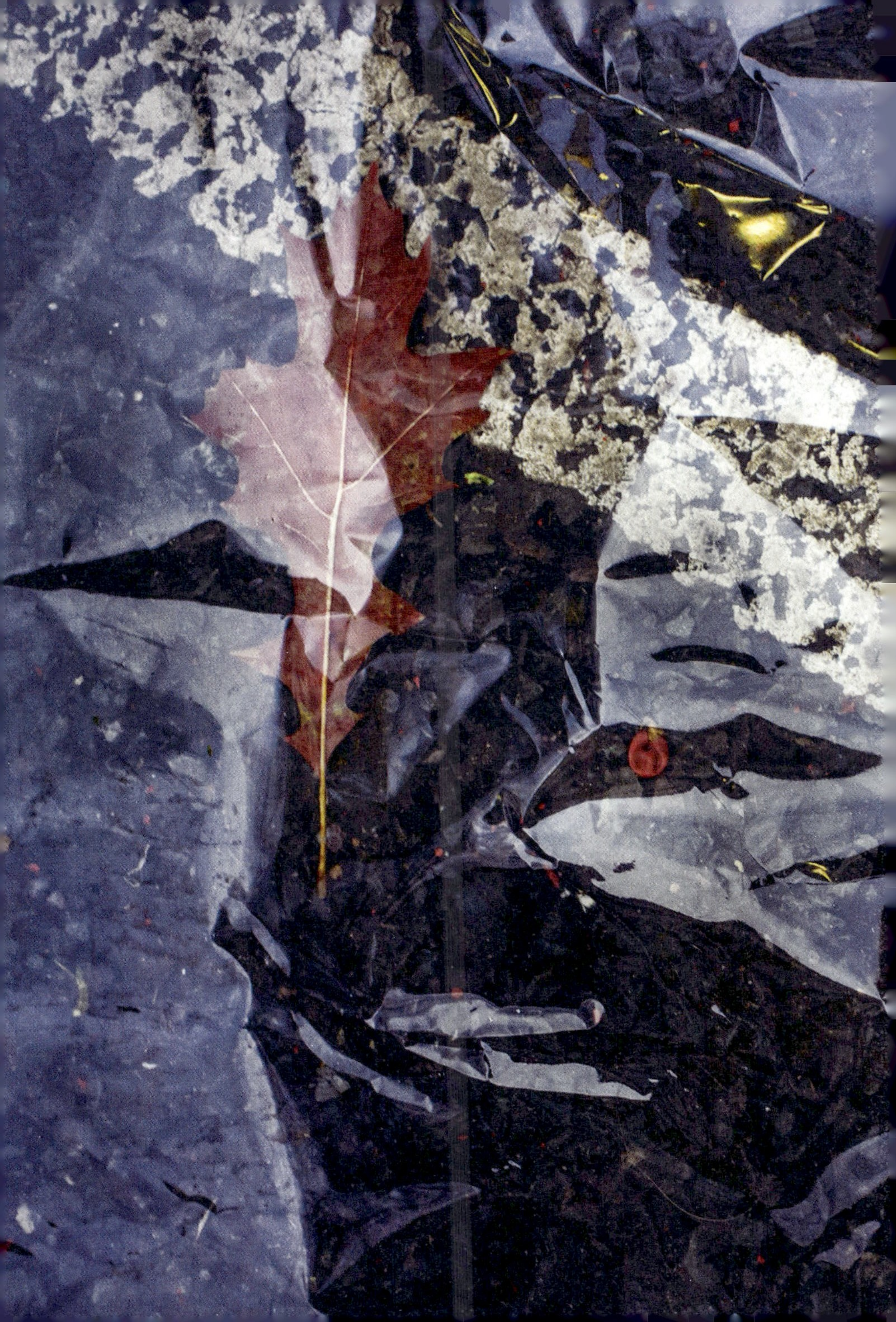

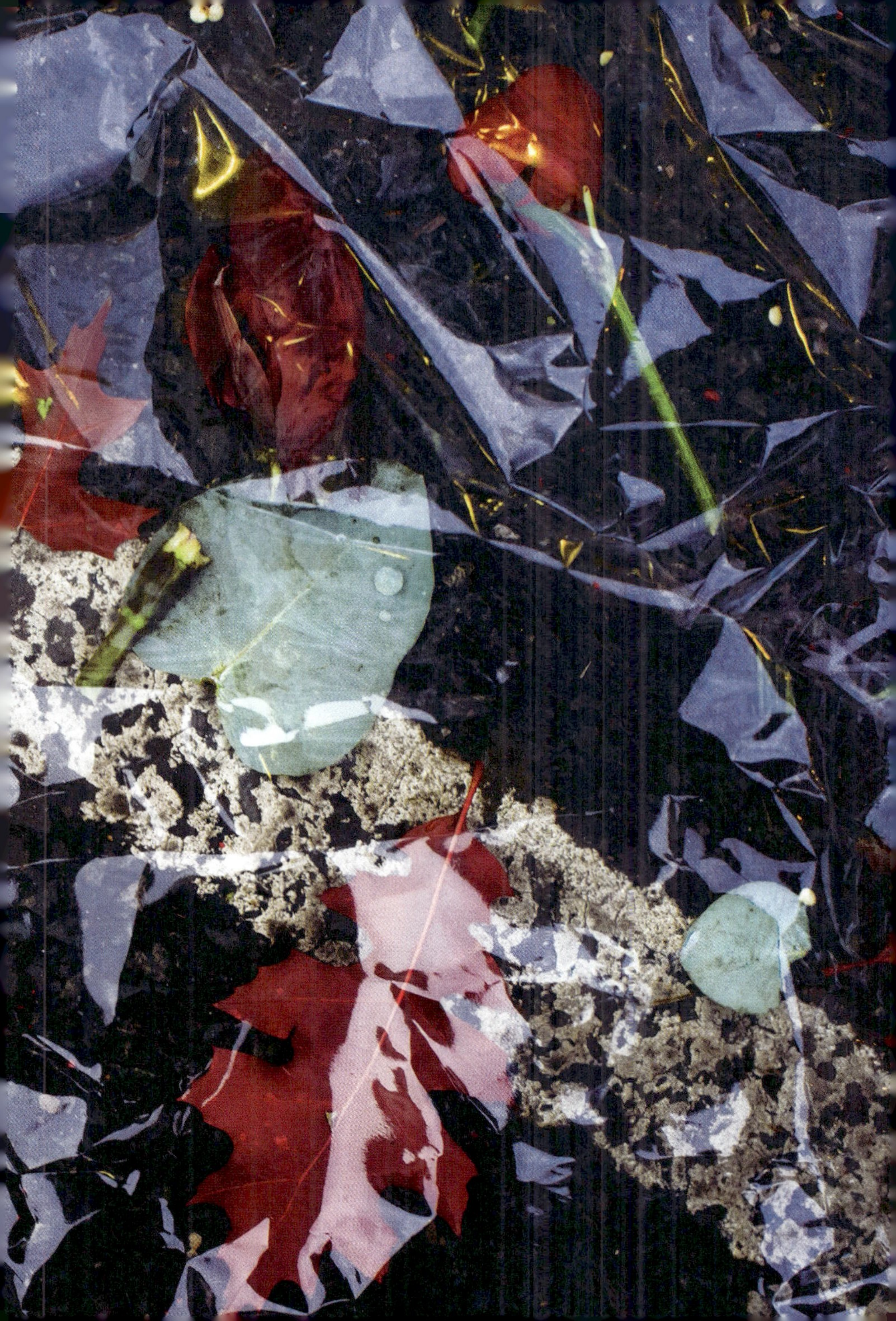

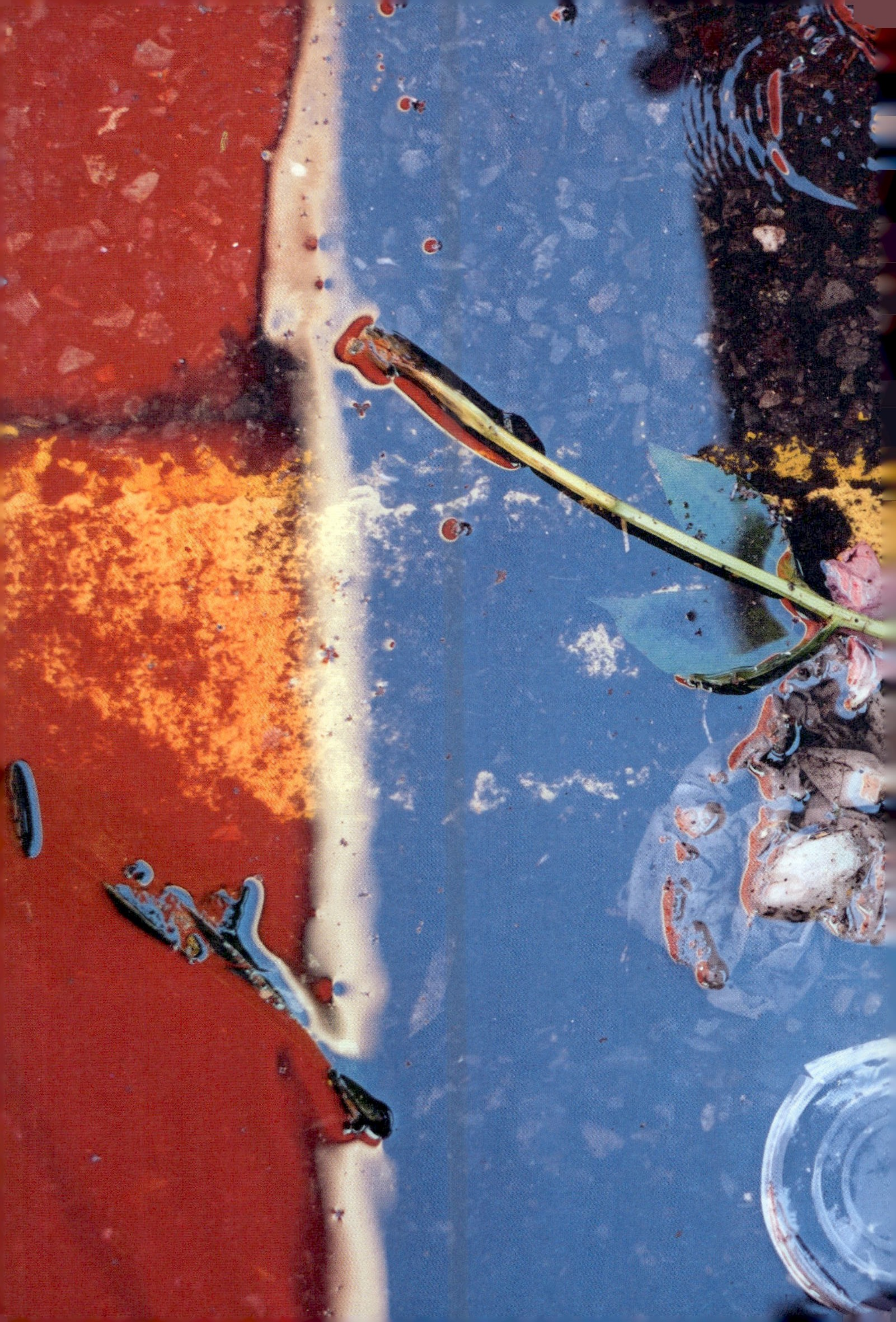

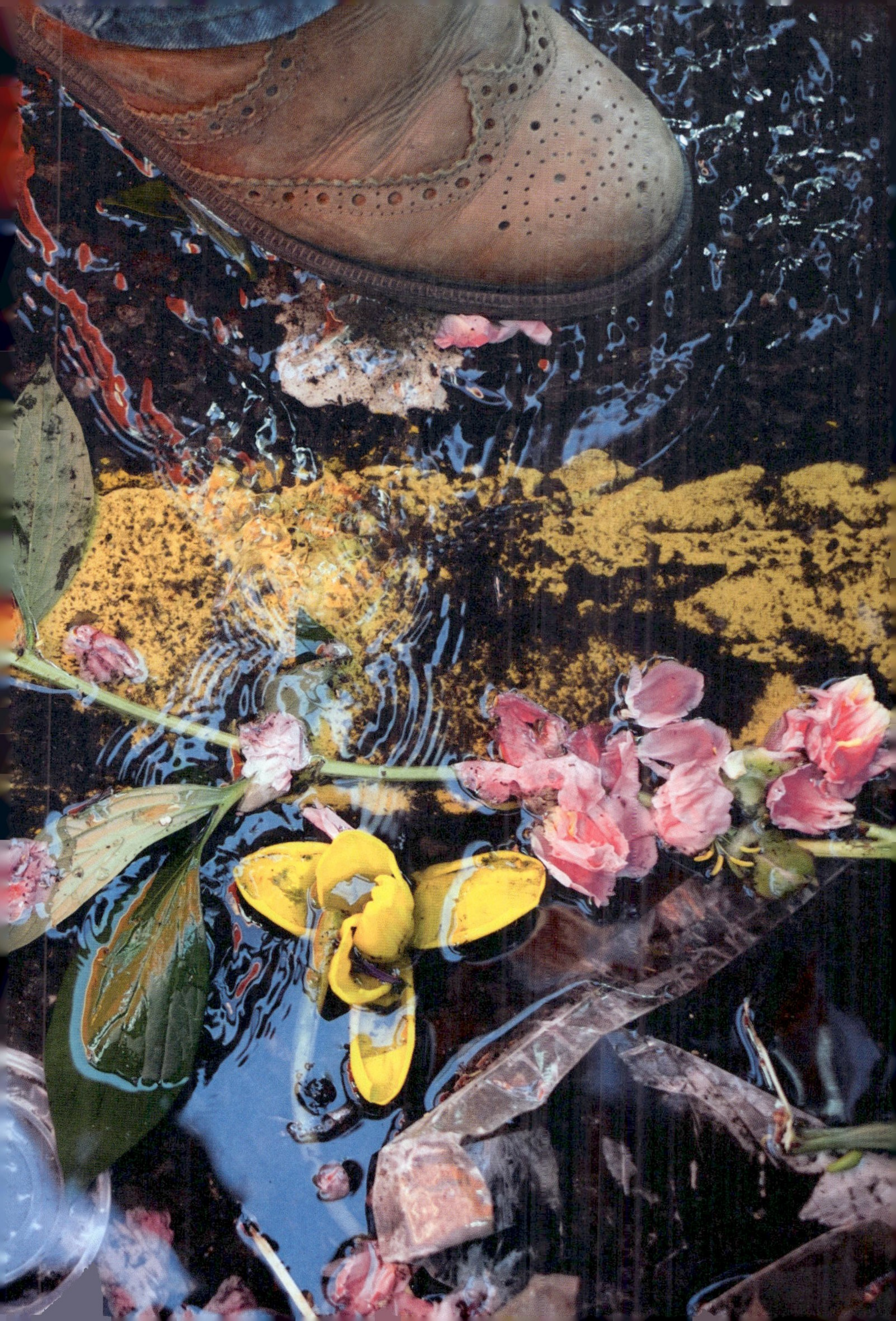

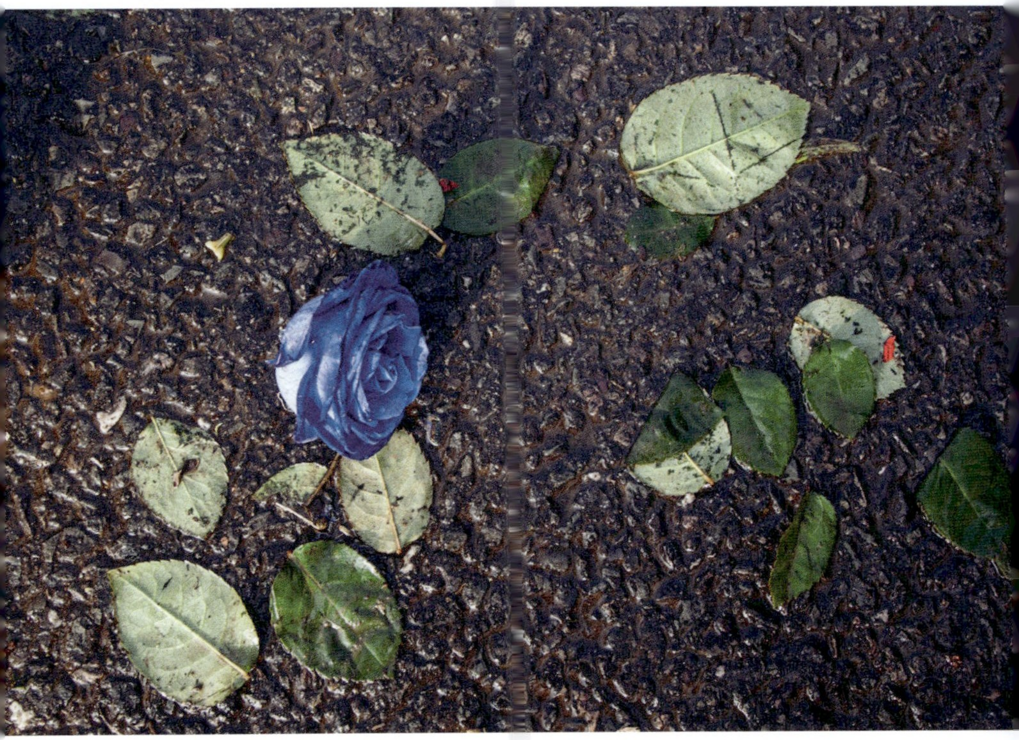

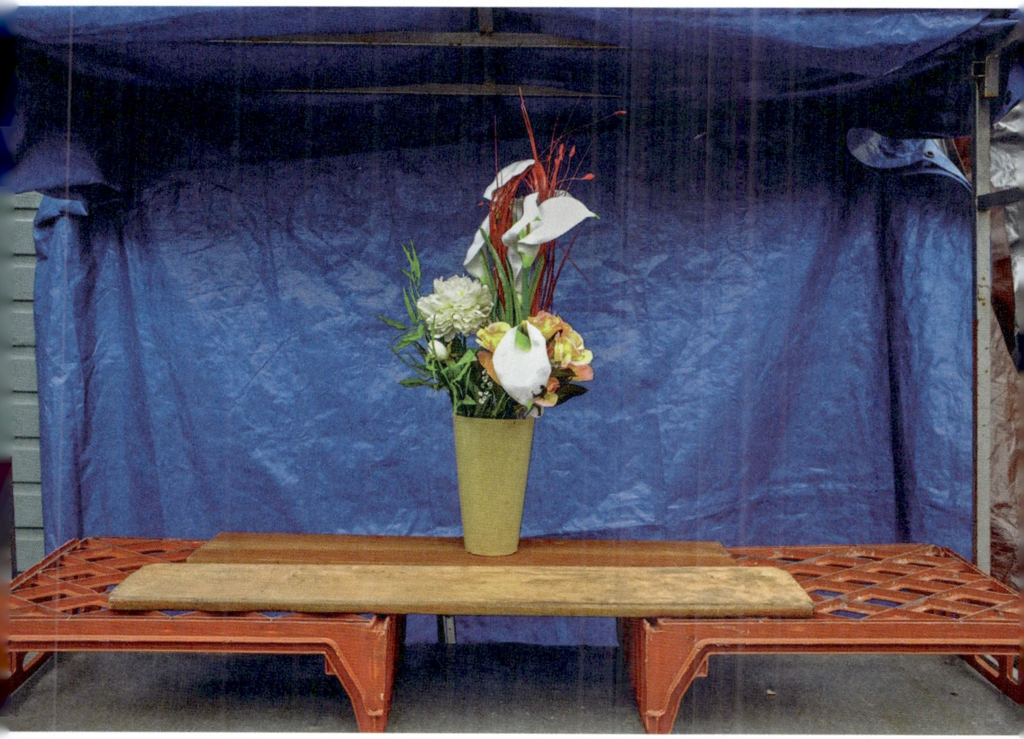

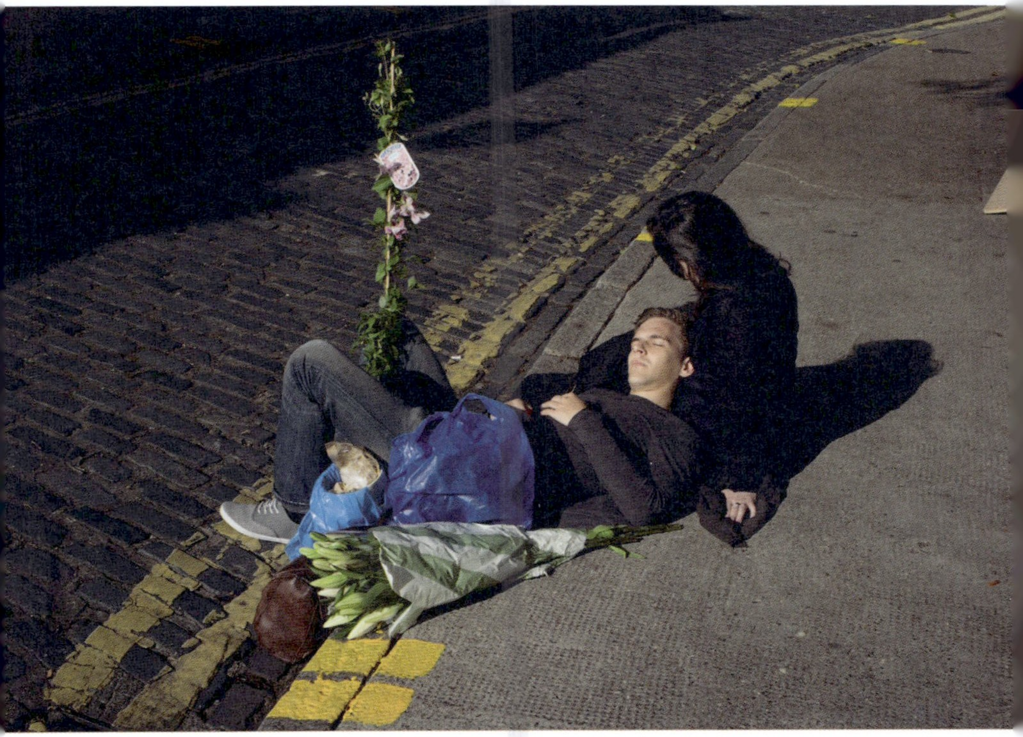

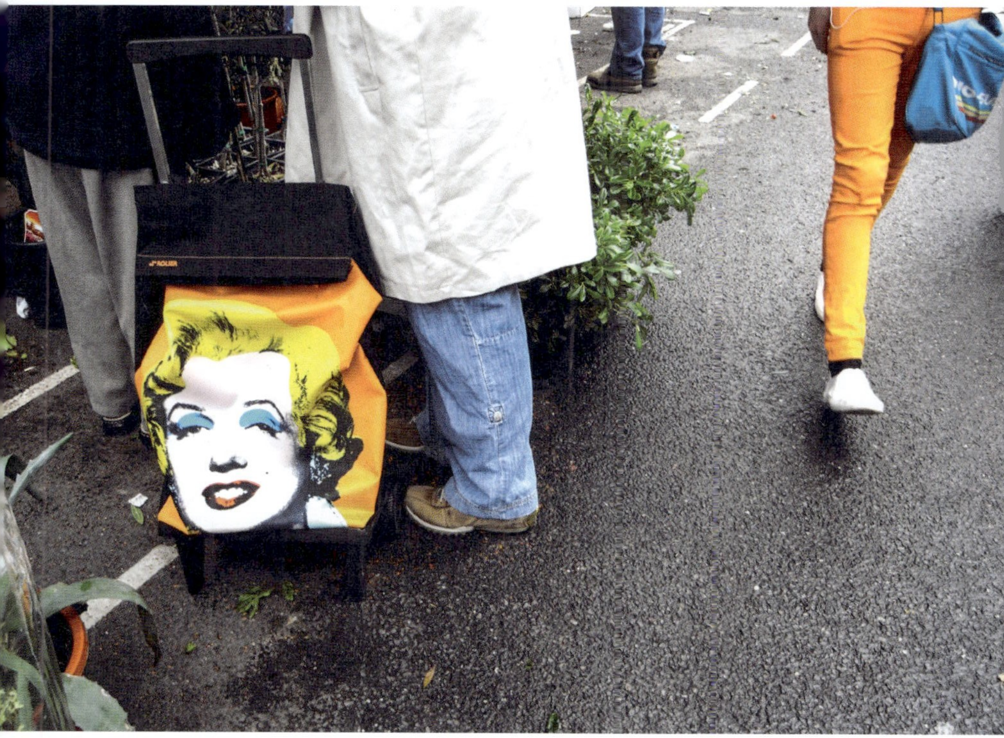

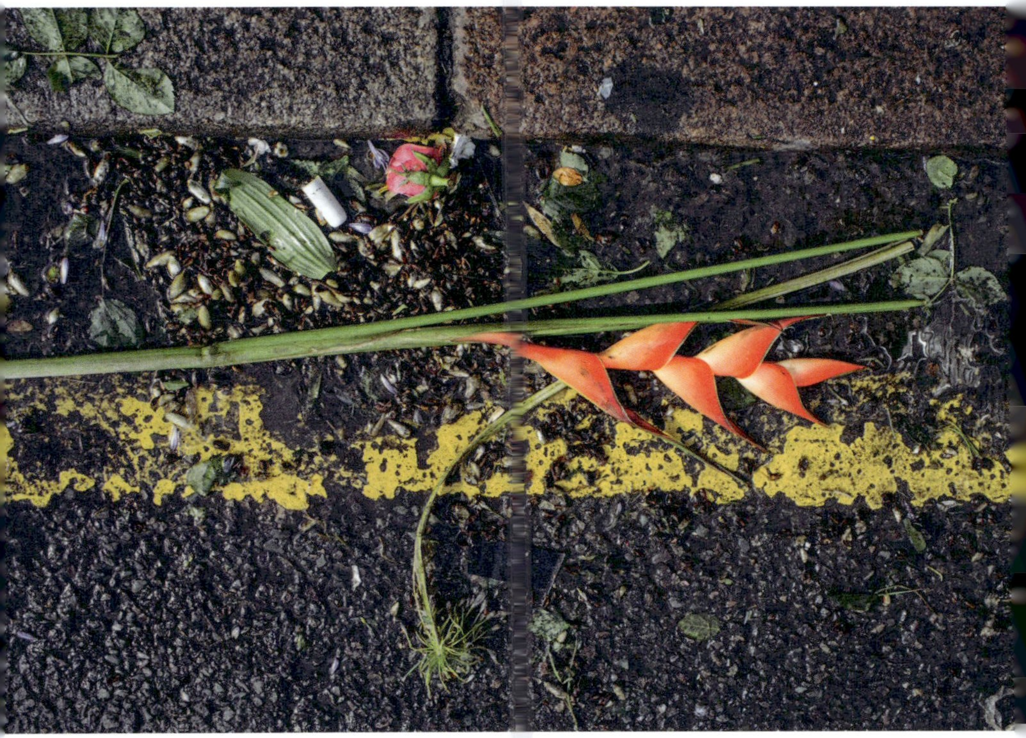

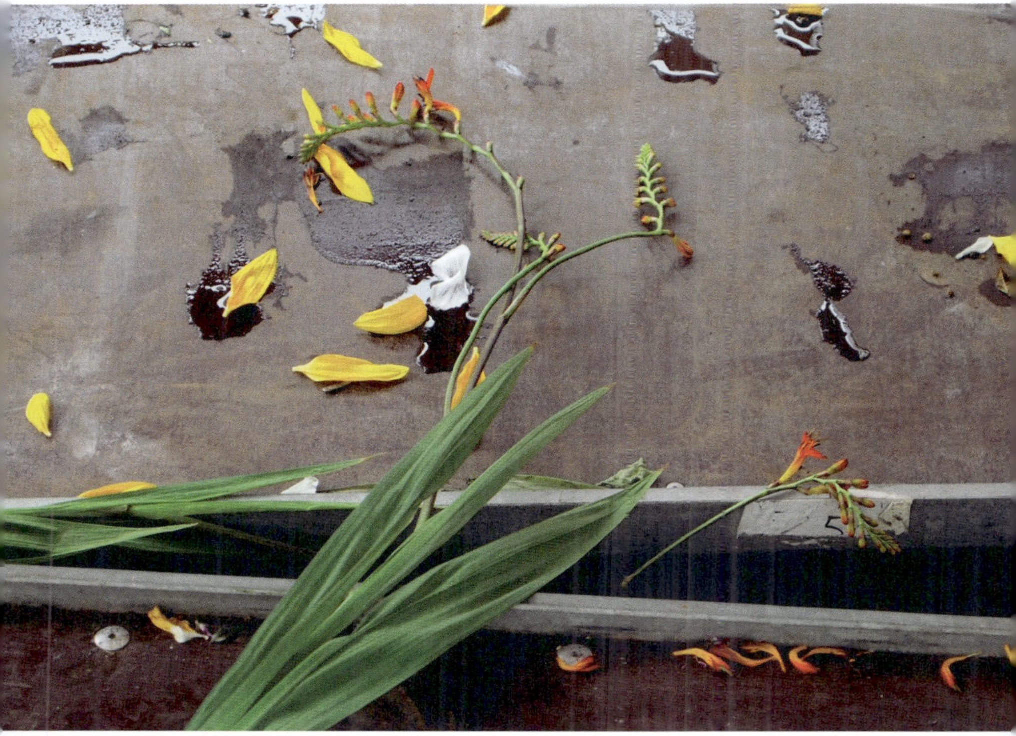

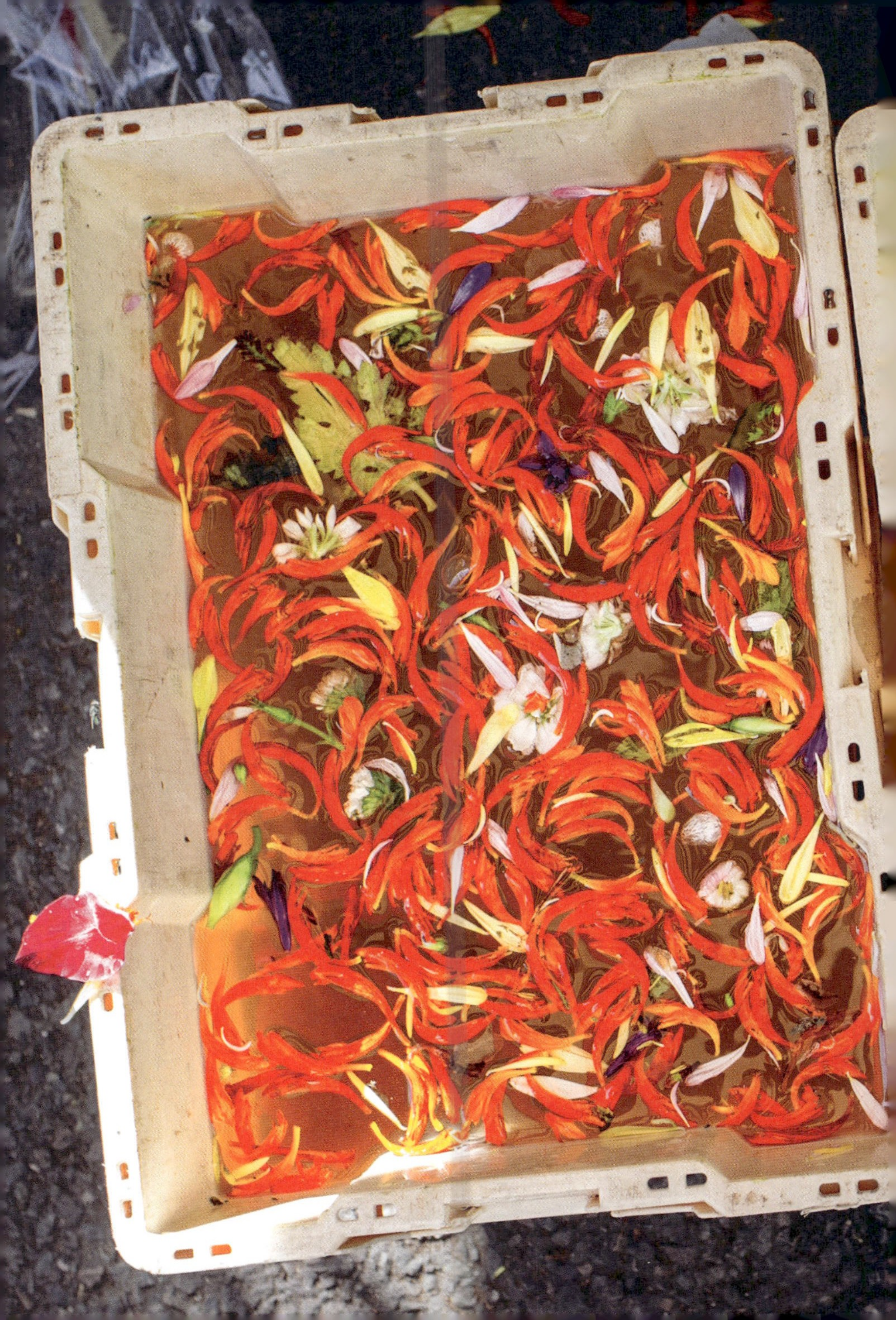

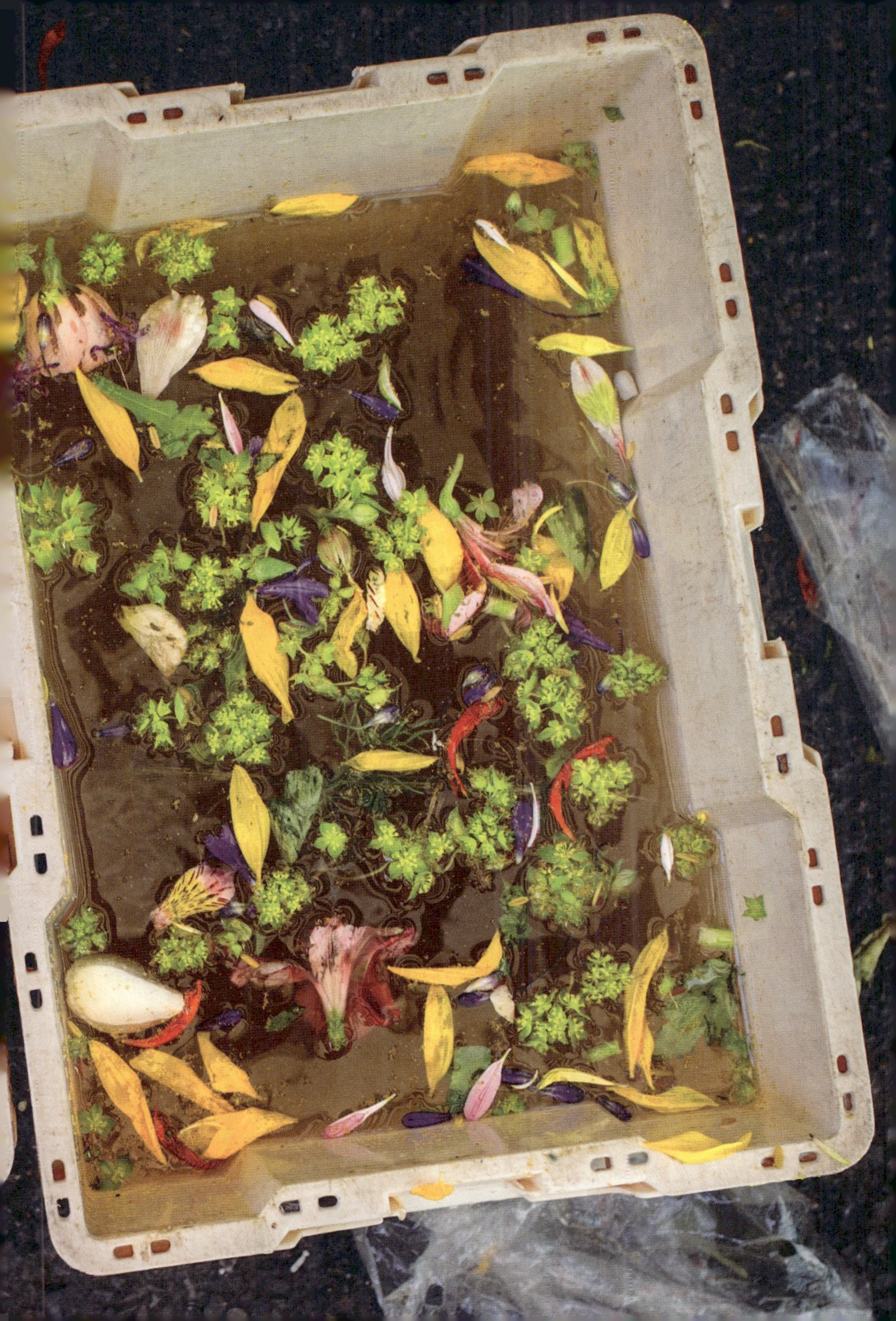

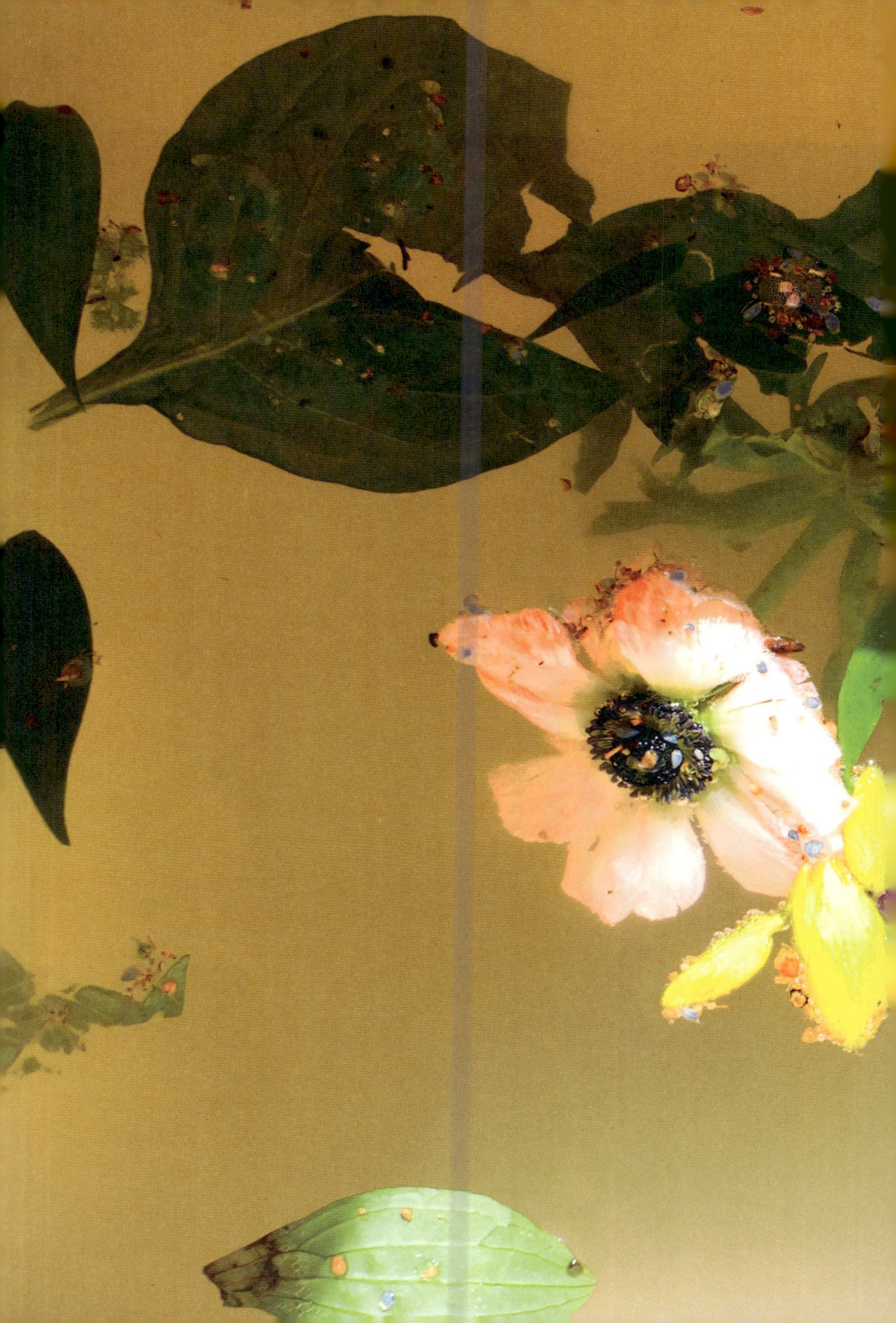

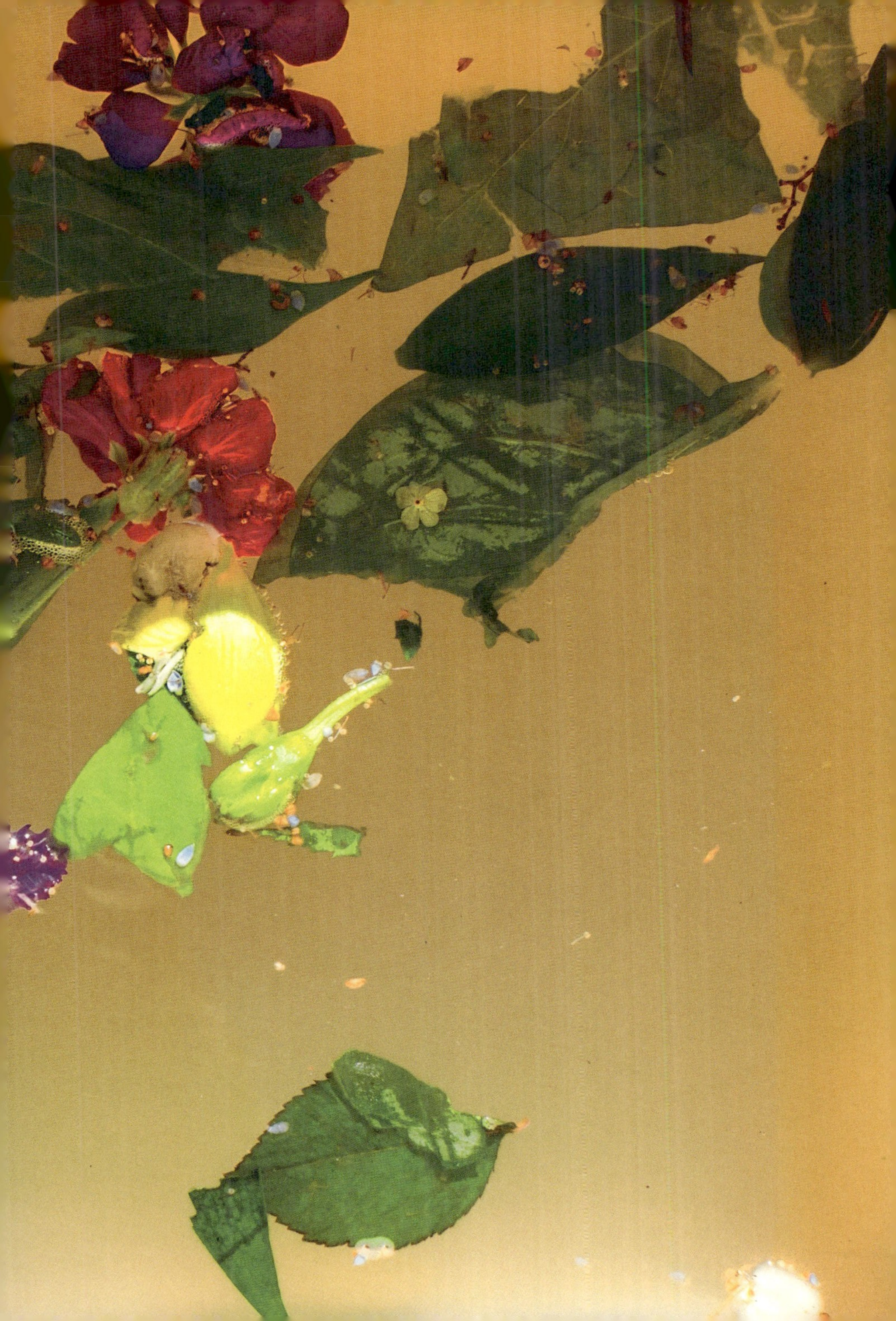

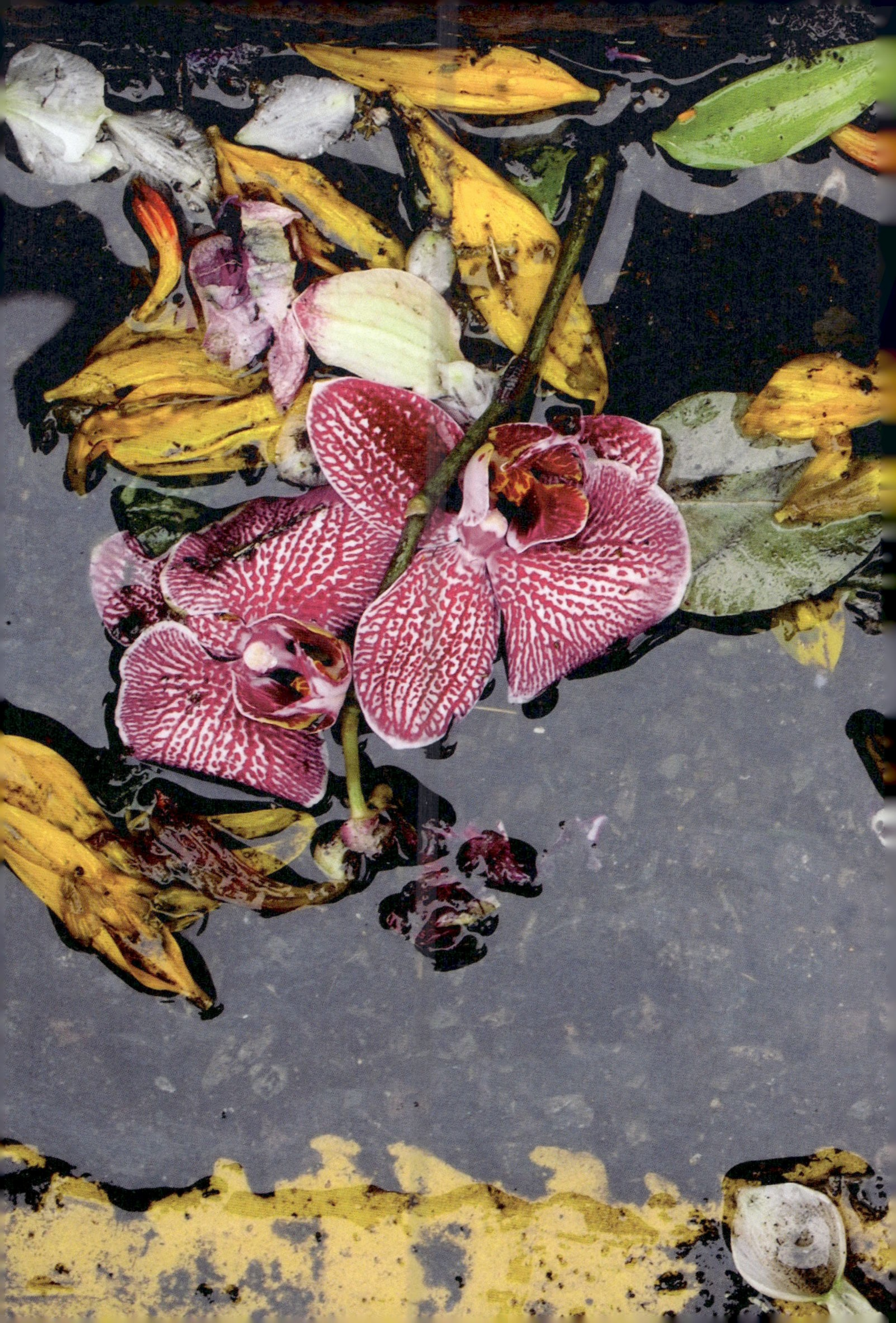

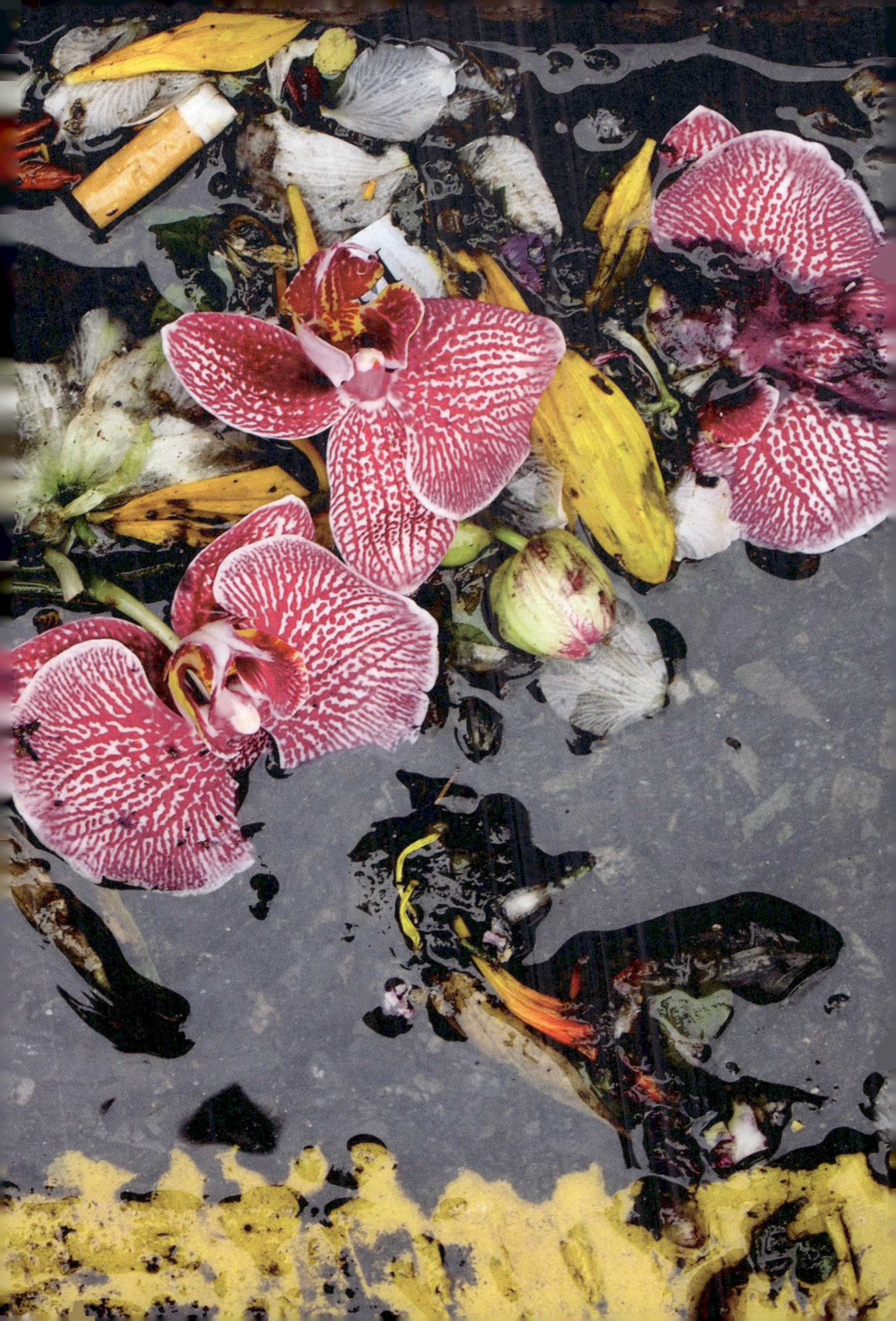

Columbia Road
First Edition

All photographs © Johanna Neurath
Design and sequence by Johanna Neurath and Hoxton Mini Press
Series design by breadcollective.co.uk

A CIP catalogue record for this book is available from the British Library.

ISBN: 978-1-910566-01-5

First published in the United Kingdom in 2015 by Hoxton Mini Press

Printed and bound by: WKT, China

To order books, collector's editions and signed prints please go to:
www.hoxtonminipress.com